GREAT PARTIES for KIDS

Over 35 Celebrations for Toddlers to Preteens

Nancy Fyke

Lynn Nejam

Vicki Overstreet

Williamson Publishing Company

Charlotte, Vermont 05445

Library of Congress Cataloging-in-Publication Data

Fyke, Nancy, 1950-
    Great parties for kids:
over 35 celebrations for toddlers to preteens / by Nancy Fyke, Lynn Nejam & Vicki Overstreet.
        p.   cm.
    ISBN 0-913589-82-9
    1. Children's parties.   I. Nejam, Lynn, 1953- .
II. Overstreet, Vicki, 1948- . III. Title.
GV1205.F95 1994   94-380
793.2'1—dc20   CIP

Cover design: Trezzo-Braren Studio
Interior design: Marie Owen
Illustrations: Chuck Galey
Printing: Capital City Press

Williamson Publishing Co.
Box 185, Charlotte, Vermont 05445
1-800-234-8791

Manufactured in the United States of America

10 9 8 7 6 5 4 3 2 1

We dedicate this book to our parents:

    Otho and Dot Johnson
    Glenn and June Harkins
    Vince and Kitty Rueseler

And present it as a gift to our children:

    Earl, Joel, and Georgia
        Fyke
    Loris, Brooke, Haley, and
        Avery Nejam
    Leah and William Overstreet

And thank our husbands for their patience and understanding:

    Dr. F. Earl Fyke III
    Mr. A. Waddell Nejam
    Mr. James S. Overstreet, Jr.

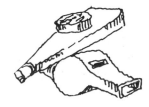

CONTENTS

"It's not my birthday, I just want to say, I miss you and want you to come over and play."

Date _____
Time _____
Location _____

Host _____   R.S.V.P. _____

MEMORIES

"How could I ever forget that moment?" We've all spoken these exact words and we've all forgotten wonderful never-to-come-again snippets of life.

Don't rely only on your memory to recall birthdays and special events in your family. Write them down.

You may wish to remember guest lists, activities, favorite gifts, favors, funny things that happened, or the funny things that were said. Write them down. The party will be over and gone tomorrow.

This book is about creating memories: the smell of a new box of crayons, the family dog tiptoeing around the china and silver on the dining room table and devouring the freshly baked birthday cake, or raking leaves and jumping in them over and over again. What would our lives be without these wonderful memories?

We appreciate the memories that make our families unique. They are the instant replay of shared times together, of times that gave us a sense of belonging.

Some memories "just happen"; others we work hard to create. Daily life becomes special with a little creativity and planning. We want to encourage you to make special memories for your children. The first step in doing that, perhaps, is to think about the fond memories from your own childhood. What family times can you recall?

Here are some of ours:

(1) Interviewing grandparents. Tape or video an interview of your child with his/her grandparents. Parent and child should make up questions before the interview.

(2) Unfamiliar transportation. Make arrangements to ride a bus, train or taxi with your child.

(3) Date with a parent. Quality time for preteen daughter or son with Dad or Mom.

(4) Mother/daughter or father/son night out. This can be started at an early age.

(5) Christmas tree forts built from discarded trees collected from neighbors.

(6) Smells. Grandmother's house; freshly baked cookies timed for child's arrival home from school.

(7) Catching fireflies.

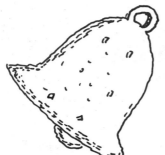
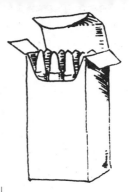

(8) Singing in the car while traveling. Do you know these songs? *I've Been Working on the Railroad, O Susannah, Frog Went a Courtin', Skidamarink, John Jacob Jingleheimer Schmidt, She'll Be Comin' 'Round the Mountain.*

(9) Taking a penny walk. Toss a penny; heads you go right, tails you go left.

(10) Drive-in movies. Talk about entertainment from your childhood.

(11) Having cherry pie or cherry pudding on George Washington's birthday, lighting the candles and singing "Happy Birthday, George."

(12) Flying a kite, playing kick the can, hop-scotch, jacks, and jump rope. Don't let those games be forgotten!

(13) Making homemade Christmas presents, wrapping paper, Christmas cards or decorations.

(14) Making snow ice cream.

(15) Family card games such as Spit, Hearts, Spoon, Battle, and Slap-Jack.

(16) Puzzles. A great family activity for vacations or holidays.

(17) Reading favorite books aloud in the evening.

(18) The annual "pilgrimage" to the beach, the mountains or your favorite retreat.

(19) Making apple crisp in the fall, with the scent of cinnamon in the air.

(20) Rocking on the front porch with grandparents and hearing the family stories for the first time.

Snow Ice Cream

4 cups clean snow
1 cup whole milk
1/4 cup sugar
1 teaspoon vanilla

Stir ingredients together in a bowl.
Eat immediately.
Serves 2.

Apple Crisp

6 large apples,
   peeled and sliced
1/4 cup water
1/2 teaspoon cinnamon
1 teaspoon lemon juice

Topping:
1 cup brown sugar
3/4 cup flour
1 cup margarine

Place apples in a greased 8"- or 9"-square pan. Add the water, then sprinkle on cinnamon and lemon juice.
Mix the margarine, flour, and brown sugar with your hands until crumbly. Sprinkle over the apples. Bake at 350° for 30 minutes.
Serves 8.

GETTING STARTED: Helpful Hints

Include your child in the party planning, the preparation (invitations, party favors, hosting or hostessing, baking the cake) and in the clean up.

Have a Pippi Longstocking birthday party. Photograph your child dressed as Pippi: hair in braids, short, loose-fitting dress, and striped stockings. Photocopy and use for the invitations.

To create parties your children and you will both enjoy and remember, focus on seven areas important to organizing a successful party.

(1) Theme

A central idea simplifies party planning, gives a feeling of unity and creates an exciting atmosphere. Build the theme around something special to your child—a toy, a hero or an activity. Themes can be seasonal or deliberately out-of-season like Christmas in July. Dress-up/costume parties are hits with both girls and boys.

The ideal time to begin planning is two weeks in advance. This is not always possible, so be flexible and use whatever time you have wisely. Include your child in the planning when possible. But remember, too much anticipation ahead of time for the child might present problems.

(2) Guest List

A good rule of thumb in determining the number of guests for young children's parties is to invite the number equal to the birthday child's age plus one. Evaluate your preschool child: what can he or she handle and what would be best for him or her. You're inviting tears with too much confusion or too many children drawing attention away from the birthday child.

When determining the number of guests for a party for school-age children, consider the space available. Will the party be indoors or outdoors?

Be sensitive to possible hurt feelings. Avoid leaving out one or two children in a classroom. Unless you invite every child, do not pass out invitations in class.

Don't try to be a superparent. Ask friends, relatives or teenagers to assist. One helper per six children works well. Be sure to inform each of his or her responsibilities.

(3) **Invitations**

The invitation is the first impression and introduction to the party. Make it fun and exciting! Start the party's theme with the invitation. This can be accomplished by using clever poems, handmade or hand-delivered invitations. Include your child in the fun! Photograph your child dressed in costume to carry out the party's theme. The photo can be photocopied in color at most print shops. Print party details on reverse side of card.

Be sure to include the honoree, host or hostess, location including address, beginning and ending times, date and rain date if needed, your phone number, and R.S.V.P. or Regrets Only. If an exact head count is important, requesting a response by a certain date allows you the freedom to call any guest not heard from a few days before the party. Teach your child to reply to invitations at an early age.

Mention any special information, such as something to bring or wear to the party, the time you will be leaving your home for a special activity, or if the children will be delivered home at the end of the party.

Be sure to send out the invitations so that they will be received one week before the party. This is adequate time for parents to arrange transportation and purchase a gift, but not so long that the invitation may be misplaced or forgotten.

The invitations in this book are patterns to use "as is" or to modify using your own creativity. Feel free to reproduce them for your personal use (see page 100).

Party length: The best parties are short. One hour is a long time for 2- and 3-year-olds and plenty of time for 4- through 6-year-olds. Depending on the planned activities for older children, an hour and a half is adequate for most parties. A rare exception is having a seated dinner that may require two hours. Better for the children to leave while they are still having a good time, than after they have become bored and uncontrollable.

Canceling the party: If the birthday child is ill, especially with a contagious disease such as chicken pox, you should postpone the party. If in doubt, consult with your pediatrician. Enlist the help of a friend to phone the guests to reschedule.

*RAIN, RAIN,
WHY TODAY?!!!*

You need a contingency plan for any party scheduled outdoors. Be prepared to move inside if the weather spoils your original party plans.

Collect a bag of supplies, equipment and prizes necessary for several inside games and activities. An appropriate video is a welcome addition to your rain emergency bag.

You hope the emergency bag is never needed, but you'll be thankful this possibility was addressed if the rain begins falling shortly before or even after your guests arrive.

Frosting a Crumbly Cake:

When cutting a cake into a shape such as a fish or fire engine, first freeze the sheet cake. This makes cutting easier and produces fewer crumbs that can present messy problems when applying the icing. To further prevent crumbs, make and apply a glaze.

Crumbly Cake Glaze

1/2 cup icing
3 tablespoons water

Heat ingredients and stir until smooth. Brush a thin layer of glaze over cake to seal crumbs. Allow glaze to dry and ice cake as desired.

Decorate a kindergarten circus party with cardboard circus displays from a local grocery or craft store. Attach colorful helium balloons to the display and place it outside the house or school building to welcome the children.

(4) Favors

Not all parties require a favor. For parties that are simply fun get-togethers, favors are optional. On the other hand, young children attending birthday parties look forward to going home with a favor. As the birthday child and guests get older and party activities are more elaborate and costly, favors are unnecessary; the party itself is the favor.

If you give favors, try to relate them to the party theme. Bandannas are big hits for a pirate party and can be used as play props during the party. For a Fun-in-the-Sun party, hats, sunglasses and blow-up beach balls help carry out the theme.

Favor bags are always well-received. The "bag" could be a brightly colored sack, a personalized plastic cup, a waffle cone, a cookie tin or any container that will hold your mixture of treats and small trinkets collected from drug stores, art/craft stores, or discount stores. We suggest stickers, magic tricks, candies, pencils and sample-sized items.

The wise party-giver has extra treats and favors available for unexpected guests or siblings. Have favors easily accessible to departing guests. Encourage the birthday child's assistance in handing out favors as good-byes and thank-yous are expressed.

(5) Food

No party would be complete without food and plenty of it! Plan the food to reflect the party theme.

For toddlers, bite-size food is easiest to handle, such as small cookies, mini-sandwiches and cupcakes.

Since young children often come dressed in their best clothes, consider a beverage that doesn't stain.

School-age children love cake! Have a sheet cake large enough to allow for "seconds," decorated with the theme of the party.

Teenagers love small bottled drinks with straws and they like to prepare their own foods, such as taco salad, baked potatoes with assorted toppings, hamburgers, hot dogs.

Homemade cakes made with love often are more special to your child than elaborate bakery cakes. We have suggested simple cake designs with each party to encourage you to make a special memory.

Be sure the kids don't fill up on sugary foods during the party. Too much sugar may lead to stomachaches or cause everyone to become too wild.

(6) Decorations

Set a festive tone and carry out the theme of the party with your decorations. Identify your home or party site with a birthday banner, balloons attached to the lamp post or mailbox, or a door decoration.

Watch for food or retail store product displays that might tie into your party theme. These may sometimes be acquired for the asking as they are often discarded after use.

Butcher paper or paper tablecloths to cover tables are great for parties; paper products make for quick clean up. Check party stores for the many designs that might enhance your theme.

Wherever possible, allow your child to participate in the decorating process.

(7) Activities and Games

Activities that are suitable to the age and number of party guests cannot be overemphasized. Plan more games than are needed, but don't feel compelled to use them all. Keep in mind that all children may not want to participate. Adult supervision of each game and activity is advisable.

Always plan a simple opening activity that children can enjoy while waiting for everyone to arrive. For small children, this might be coloring on a butcher paper-covered table, creating with play dough, using sidewalk chalk, or stringing circle-shaped fruit cereal or candies for a necklace. Older children enjoy decorating their own cupcakes, making a banner for the birthday child, or being outfitted to go along with the party theme. Background music and snacks are good ice breakers as guests arrive.

Be sure to plan some games that can be played inside or outside, depending on the weather.

Photos and Videos

You can enjoy these special events for years to come if you save the memories with photos or videos. Here are some hints:

(1) Assign someone else to do the photographing or taping during the party. You'll be busy with other things; and you will want to be in some of the pictures.

(2) Be sure your photographer knows who and what activities you want recorded. Let him or her know the schedule of events.

(3) Make sure the assigned person is familiar with your equipment. Your friend may prefer to use his or her own equipment; in that case, be sure to supply the correct film.

(4) Check your supplies—film, video tape, batteries—and test your camera and flash at least a day before the party.

(5) Don't let the photography intrude on the fun of the party.

10

Consider the amount of space you have available when planning games for the party. You may risk frustrations, even injury, if there's not enough space to move and play with lots of elbow room.

Toddlers have a short attention span, so keep games short and simple. Singing games, circle games and finger-play games are suitable for very young children.

Non-competitive games are best for children under age seven. This age has not yet gained an understanding that allows them to see another child win. Either give everyone a prize for participating or simple applause.

Children seven and older are more patient and have longer attention spans. They like to divide into teams to play games. They love races, relays, soccer, baseball, and scavenger and treasure hunts. This age is able to handle winning and losing.

When entertaining teens, have plenty of helpers. Adults set the tone for the party as they greet each guest with a handshake and a gracious welcome. We recommend several chaperons for boy-girl parties. Parents need to be visible. Older teens are great helpers if their jobs are well defined. Planned activities are essential. As with any age group, rules need to be defined and enforced. Excessive idle time is not advisable.

To relate the games to the theme of your party, change the names of your games to fit, such as "Hot Potato Kryptonite" for a Super Hero Party or "Pin the Hat on the Witch" for a Halloween Party.

With each party idea we have suggested specific games that are appropriate for the ages indicated for that particular party. Use the index to find other games and activities. You may also wish to check with your child's preschool or gym teacher for games that the children enjoy and know how to play. From these suggestions let your child help select the games to be played. Be sure you and your child are familiar with the rules and all necessary equipment is on hand.

PARTIES *for* 2- to 6-Year-Olds

Crayon Party

Guest List: Ages 2 to 5. Be sure to have a couple of teen helpers.

Invitations: Purchase one 8-pack box of crayons for each guest. Tie the crayons with ribbon, curling the ribbon with a pair of shears. Save these for favors. Place the folded invitation in the crayon box and seal with a sticker. Hand deliver invitation. (See page 101.)

Favors: Place tissue paper in primary-colored plastic cup. Add candy and tied crayons. Print each child's name on cup.

Food: Bake a sheet cake and frost it white. Using bright colors, print the name of each guest on the cake's top. Add brightly colored candles. Or, frost a sheet cake bright yellow. Decorate like a box of crayons.

Decorations: Use white paper for a tablecloth. Let the guests color during the party on the tablecloth. Use paper products in primary colors.

About Balloons

Balloons are inappropriate for parties with kids under 3 years of age or when younger siblings are present. Little ones may put balloon pieces in their mouths, causing them to choke. Also avoid candies wrapped in foil with toddlers—another favorite for them to swallow.

ZACH CRAYONS

It's a birthday of colors
You're sure to have fun
Lots of games and surprises
We'll play till we're done!
Wear your favorite color
And come with a smile
We'll look like a rainbow
And have fun all the while.
So connect all the dots
And the name you'll find out
Of a SPECIAL birthday person
Of that there's no doubt.

TIME:

DATE:

PLACE:

R.S.V.P.

Activities/Games:

(1) *Color a Tablecloth:* Have table covered with butcher paper. Children color paper with crayons until all guests arrive.

(2) *Self-Portraits:* Before the party, cut a piece of butcher paper the size of a child for each guest. Have children lie on individual pieces of paper, slick side down. Helper traces child's complete body shape. Child colors in own clothes, hair, and features.

(3) *Sidewalk Art:* Children draw pictures on the sidewalk or driveway using colorful chalk.

Hints:

When making self-portraits, be sure children spread fingers apart and turn their feet side to side so the helper can draw around them. The helper should put the chin line and hair line on the drawings, too.

Discuss with the children their clothing and facial features. "Are there stripes on your shirt? What color are your eyes? hair? Are you wearing a watch or necklace? Are your fingernails painted?"

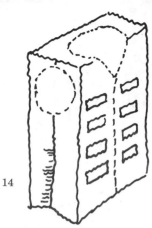

Stop, Look & Listen Party

Preschoolers bring their favorite riding toy and safety helmet for fun and safety tips.

Guest List: Ages 2 to 5. Be sure to have several teen helpers.

Invitations: See page 101.

Favors: Vest with reflective tape, horns, bike reflectors, miniature cars.

Food: Decorate sheet cake with traffic light on one end of cake top with red, yellow, and green lights. Print message "STOP, LOOK, LISTEN. It's (birthday child)'s Birthday!" on other end of the cake top.

Decorations: Use checkered flags, red, yellow, and green crepe paper streamers, and balloons to decorate party site. Attach red, yellow, and green helium-filled balloons to traffic cones.

Vest Pattern:

1. Draw vest pattern in the shape shown in diagram on brown grocery bag. Cut out around the dotted lines.
2. Glue on reflective tape across front and back.

Making the Cake:

1. Bake a 9" x 13" cake. After it has cooled, frost it smooth. Use yellow frosting for the sides and chocolate for the top.
2. Make the outline of a traffic light using yellow frosting.
3. Ice three large cookies —red, yellow, and green for the lights. Let icing dry. Place on the cake.
4. Light covers: Cut circle shapes the same size as the cookies out of Fancy Foil® or aluminum foil. Fold circle in half and glue. Push straight edge into cake, curving around cookie.

STOP, LOOK & LISTEN

Happy Birthday!

Activities/Games:

(1) *Obstacle Course:* Make course using traffic cones or empty coffee cans to which you have tied helium-filled balloons. The first cone should be 20 yards from the starting line and additional cones about 10 feet apart. Rider follows course, zigzagging from the right of one cone to the left of the next, and so on. Stagger the starting time of each child. This is not a race! Use teen helpers to keep traffic flowing in one direction.

(2) *Red Light, Green Light*: Determine a start and finish line. "It" (the birthday child at first) stands at the finish line. The other players line up 50 feet away at the starting line. The object is for the players to walk toward "It" while his or her back is turned as he or she counts to 10. At "10," the child yells, "Red light!" and turns quickly. Any player who is moving when "It" turns must go back to the starting line. "It" shouts "Green light!" and the game continues. The first player to reach the finish line and touch "It" is the next "It."

(3) *Safety Talk:* Have a friendly, uniformed police officer speak on bicycle safety and teach bicycle hand signals.

This is an outside party so be sure to have a rain date or an alternate indoor party site such as a gymnasium or large recreation room.

Dinosaur Party

Guest List: Ages 2 to 6.

Invitations: Hand deliver colored plastic egg with invitation and plastic or gummy dinosaur inside. (See page 102.)

Favors: Dinosaur-shaped sponges, dinosaur stickers, puzzles or magnets, removable dinosaur tattoos.

Food: Stegosaurus cake and dino egg ice cream.

Decorations: Make a centerpiece using plants, moss, plastic dinosaur figures, and candy eggs. Using acrylic paint and dinosaur-shaped sponges, print a border on a solid color paper or cloth tablecloth. Position a large dinosaur (blow up water toy, stuffed animal, or painted cardboard box) in the front yard. Tie balloons around its neck to welcome guests. Place dinosaur footprints made from colored construction paper leading to party site.

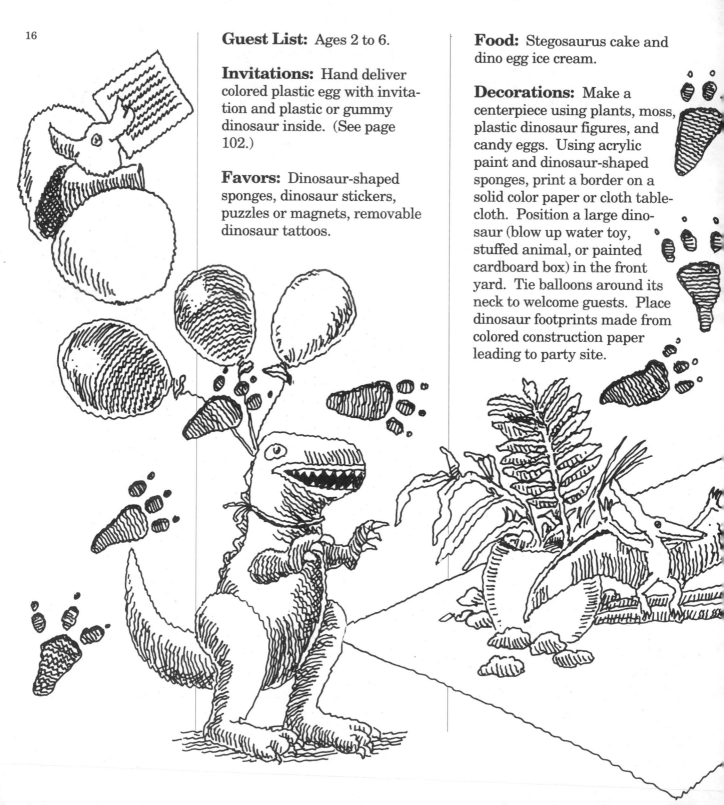

Activities/Games:

(1) *Fossil Hunt:* Hide small plastic dinosaur toys in the sand. Use a sandbox, if available, or fill a small wading pool with sand. Cover until time for the game. Let children gather around and hunt for the "fossils." Make sure that everyone gets at least one to keep.

(2) *Dino-Bone Hunt:* Tie a bone-shaped dog biscuit to a lollipop with a curly ribbon. Hide them in the yard so young children can easily find them.

(3) *Pin the Horn on the Triceratops:* Create a hornless triceratops drawing using the party invitation on page 102. Tape it to the wall at children's height. Before party day, make horns out of colorful construction paper. Place double-folded masking tape on back of each horn. Guests line up. Blindfold the first guest, turn the child around three times, and point the player toward the dinosaur. Then the child "pins" the horn on the triceratops.

(4) *Read Dinosaur Story Aloud:* Place quilt on the ground and gather the children in a semicircle. To keep children quiet while reading, provide individual nut cups filled with raisins or grapes. We suggest *Danny and the Dinosaur* by Syd Hoff or *The Berenstein Bears and the Missing Dinosaur Bone* by Stan and Jan Berenstein.

Have the children cut out bone shapes from construction paper and have an indoor bone hunt.

Dino Egg Ice Cream

Before the party day, scoop ice cream and roll individual scoops in colorful sprinkles. Place each scoop in a cupcake paper and freeze.

Stegosaurus Cake

Bake cake in an egg-shaped cake pan available at a cake decorating or party store. Use a lady finger or cupcake for the head. Frost body and head smooth in bright color. Make tail with frosting. For bony plates along back and down tail, decorate with two rows of citrus slice candies or sliced gumdrops. Use raisins for eyes.

Trash Bash

Trash Mix

1/4 cup margarine, melted

1 1/4 teaspoons
    seasoned salt

4 1/2 teaspoons
    Worcestershire sauce

8 cups total: corn, rice,
    and wheat waffle-
    shaped cereals

1 cup small pretzels

1 cup mixed nuts or
    peanuts

1. Combine melted butter, salt, and Worcestershire sauce.
2. Pour over remaining ingredients and mix well.
3. Transfer to open roasting pan. Bake at 250° for 1 hour, stirring every 15 minutes.
4. Cool and store in airtight container. Makes 9 cups.

Make Your Own Crayons

Make these ahead of time. Melt down old crayons (one color at a time) in a saucepan over low heat or double boiler. Pour into mini-cupcake papers. Cool. When solidified, children may use them to color. These make nice party favors.

Here's a fun party that will encourage children to become actively involved in recycling and reusing wherever they are.

Guest List: Ages 4 to 6.

Invitations: Print poem on 3½" x 5 " paper and glue inside brown paper lunch bag (size approximately 5" x 11"). Fold bag to 5" x 6". Use sticker to close. Address front and mail. (See page 102.)

Favors: Place *trash mix* (see recipe) in recyclable container (paper cup, paper sack, 8"-square cloth tied with string). Print recipe for *trash mix* on card and attach with string. Print child's name on favor. Another favor the children will love are the *Tin Can Stilts*.

Food: *Chili Bag Lunch:* Open small corn chip bag. Spoon in 1 tablespoon of chili or salsa. Add grated cheese. Eat out of bag with spoon. *Fruit Juice-on-a-Stick:* Fruit juice, small paper cups, flat wooden sticks. 1) Place the cups in a muffin pan and fill to ¾ with juice. 2) Freeze until partially set. Insert sticks. 3) Freeze. 4) Peel the paper away and eat.

Decorations: Tables covered in plain brown paper. Paint large recycle symbol in center with others on corners or border. Use hole puncher confetti, curling ribbon, and twine as accents.

Activities/Games:

(1) *Newsprint Hats:* Use a full sheet of newspaper. Fold in half before starting to fold actual hat. Proceed as in diagram. For younger children, adult needs to make one hat per child ahead of time. Children decorate using leaves, feathers, and glue.

(2) *Recycling Relay:* Two teams are formed. First child in line for each team runs to the box, grabs an item (plastic wrap, foil, cardboard, plastic container, tin soda can) and runs to opposite end to place in the correct recycle bin. Repeat for each team member. Team that first gets all items in correct box wins. (Each recycle bin should have drawing as well as printed name of correct items on it.)

(3) *Tin Can Stilts:* Children receive tin can stilt favor. Adjust strings to proper length for each child as per instructions. Children have free time to practice walking on stilts.

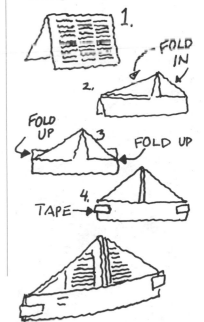

Tin Can Stilts

Use 2 same-size empty cans. Using can opener make a hole in each side. String rope or heavy twine through holes. Adjust to correct arm length. Lift and step to walk.

Newsprint Hats

Friends around the World

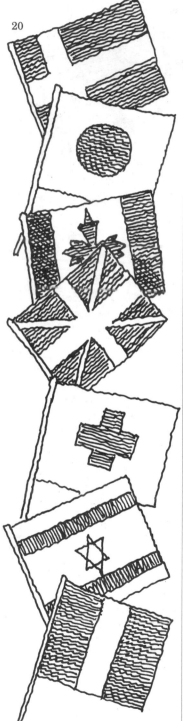

Children come to this party dressed in costume from another country. Each child brings a snack native to his/her particular country to be served at the party.

Guest List: Ages 4 to 6.

Invitations: See page 103. Make an invitation that says Happy Birthday in other languages: In Venezuela, Happy Birthday is sung as *Hoy Es Tu Dia* (oy ess too DEE-ah), or "Today is your day." In Holland, *Lang zal zij [hij] leven* (lahng sahl say [hay] LAY-vehn) is a birthday tune that means "Long may she [he] live." In Italian, Happy Birthday is *Buon Compleanno*. In Polish, Happy Birthday is *Szcześliwych, Urodzin* (stown-sleeVERH ooROgin).

Favors: Items with earth or globe motif such as pencils, pencil sharpeners, squeeze balls, erasers, yo-yos, stickers, puzzles, maps.

Food: Serve food brought by guests. For dessert, cupcakes decorated with flags from different countries or doll cake with native dress of choice (see recipe).

Decorations: Hang posters with scenes from foreign places (obtain from travel agencies). Decorate the table with dolls and flags from countries around the world. Play festive music from Spain, Mexico, Greece, or wherever.

Activities/Games:

(1) *World Fashions:* Ask a dramatic, outgoing friend to act as emcee for a fashion show. The children pair off and walk around the room as the emcee describes each outfit making every guest feel special.

(2) *Story Time:* Host parent, dressed in costume, reads an age-appropriate story about children in other countries. Examples: *The Story About Ping* by Marjorie Flack or *Madeline* by Ludwig Bemelmans.

(3) *Ciu-ciu Babka (choo-choo BOPka):* This is a children's game from Poland. "It" is blindfolded. Other children are allowed to move quietly around the room. "It" tags a person. If "It" guesses correctly the name of the person tagged, that person becomes "It."

Doll Cake

Bake cake using skirt pan, tube or bundt pan according to package instructions. Cool and turn out onto a cake plate. Insert doll or doll pick. If using tube or bundt pan, fill in space with icing or make a cardboard paper cone to fit doll's waist, tapering it into the top of the cake. Using a star tube decorate doll bodice and sleeves. Ice skirt and decorate with candy pearls, roses, or whatever to depict native costume.

Everyone Loves a Parade

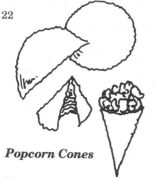

Popcorn Cones

Use a large dinner plate to draw a circle on construction paper. Cut in half across the middle. Pull straight edge together to form cone and glue. Makes 2.

Hats:

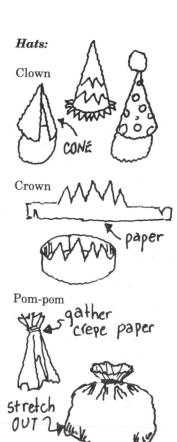

Guest List: Ages 2 to 6.

Invitations: See page 103.

Favors: Kazoos, toy flutes, toy drums, pinwheels, flags.

Food: Popcorn served in popcorn bags or handmade cones. *Drum cake:* Frost a two-layer round cake with white icing. Zigzag top and bottom edges of cake with blue icing. Use red string licorice for connecting lines, and large yellow gum drops. Print *Happy Birthday* message on top and use brightly colored candles.

Decorations: Crepe paper streamers, brightly colored paper products, parade banner with birthday child's name.

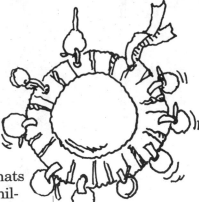

Activities/Games:

(1) *Preparations:* Before the party, gather instruments from household items. An empty coffee can or oatmeal box makes a good drum. Waxed paper wrapped around a comb makes a homemade kazoo— hold the sides of the comb to lips and hum. Sandpaper blocks and macaroni in a box are good noise makers. Use pots and pans with spoons for drums.

(2) *Parade Hats:* Provide hats for children to decorate. Children decorate hats with glitter, feathers, pom-poms, artificial flowers, fabric and trim scraps.

(3) *Follow the Leader Parade:* Wearing hats and carrying "instruments," everyone marches the same way as the leader (who is the birthday child at first). After a few minutes the next child in line becomes the leader with the first child going to the end of the line. Play this game until all have had a chance to lead.

Tambourine

Take an aluminum pie plate with holes punched around outside edge. Attach old keys and jingle bells to holes with garbage bag ties. String with curling ribbons for decorations.

These are so easy and inexpensive, kids can receive one for a party favor.

Paper Bag Maracas

Paint paper bags with bright colors. Fill with dried beans. Tie off tightly. Shake, rattle, and roll.

Use for another party favor or kids can make them for an activity.

Go Fish

Guest List: Ages 2 to 5. Remember, one helper per six children is advisable.

Invitations: Using colorful paper-by-the-pound, draw a fishing pole. Punch a hole in the card and attach string or yarn for fishing line. Sew a gummy worm to card, knotting the thread on back. (See page 104.)

Favors: Live goldfish or certificate for goldfish from pet store, gummy worms, fish sponges, bath tub toys.

Food: Ice a sheet cake with light blue icing and decorate with plastic fish. Serve punch from a goldfish bowl. Provide small bowls of fish-shaped crackers for snacking.

Decorations: Drape colored fish netting (available at most party stores) over paper tablecloth and scatter sea shells on the table. The table centerpiece could be a goldfish bowl filled with live fish. Also, pin brightly colored fish to sheet for Go Fishin' game.

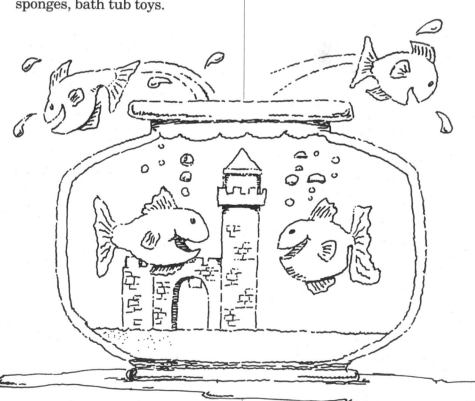

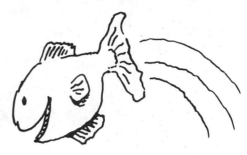

Activities/Games:

(1) *Play Dough:* Children play with play dough until all guests arrive. Different colors of play dough are fun. Also be sure to have rolling pins and cookie cutters on hand.

(2) *Go Fishin':* Put a sheet or bedspread over a fence, box or table. Hide one helper and the prizes behind the sheet. Use an old fishing pole, but replace the hook with a clothespin. Each child casts the line over the sheet and the helper attaches a prize to the clothespin. You will need a second helper out front.

Play Dough Recipe

3 cups flour
1 1/2 cups salt
6 tablespoons oil
3 teaspoons cream of tartar
3 cups water
Few drops food coloring

Mix all ingredients in a pan. Heat slowly until mixture lumps together. Remove from heat. Stir with hands or spoon until mixture is consistency of dough. Knead and store in airtight container. Dough will keep for several days if refrigerated.

Zoo Party

If you don't live near a zoo, plan a similar party at a children's museum, aquarium, or nearby farm.

Guest List: Ages 2 to 5 *and* some parents. Depending on the children's ages, the party should be small with approximately four to six children.

Invitations: When selecting a time for the party, remember this age child usually naps in the afternoon. Be sure to give a rain plan or date. (See page 105.)

Favors: Box of animal crackers, animal sponges, plastic zoo animals or an animal coloring book.

Food: Pack a simple picnic lunch of peanut butter and jelly sandwiches, animal-shaped iced sugar cookies and box drinks. Paper products are ideal for serving. Be sure to bring along quilts for seating and disposable towelettes for cleaning up.

Decorations: Put a "Happy Birthday" sign or banner at zoo entrance.

Hint: Use large animal-shaped cookie cutters to cut sandwiches.

Avery's Birthday

Activities/Games:

(1) *Copy Cat:* Arrange children in circle. Parent in center acts out an animal sound or movement to be copied by everyone. Example: roar like a lion, hop like a kangaroo, growl like a bear.

(2) *Guess Who?:* Have children take turns acting like a zoo animal. Person who guesses correctly gets to be "it."

(3) *Zoo Tour:* Parents and children can tour the zoo together going at their own speed. Check with your zoo about special tours available.

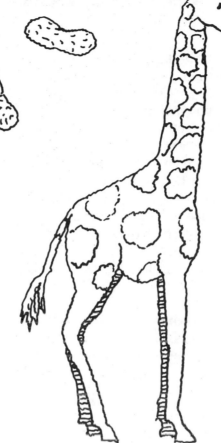

Vicki's Animal Sugar Cookies

2/3 cup margarine
1 cup granulated sugar
1 egg
2 cups flour
1/2 tsp. salt
1/2 tsp. baking soda
1 tsp. vanilla

1. Cream butter and sugar. Add egg and mix well. Sift dry ingredients together and add gradually. Add vanilla.
2. Chill in refrigerator 1 hour, then roll 1/8-inch thick.
3. Cut with animal-shaped cookie cutter.
4. Bake for 10-12 minutes at 350°. Cool.

Glaze:

2 cups confectioners' sugar
1/2 tsp. almond extract
1/4 - 1/3 cup milk

1. Mix ingredients until smooth.
2. Add food coloring for desired color.
3. Dip cooled cookies face-side down in icing, allowing excess to drip off.
4. Let dry 1/2 hour.

Fun-in-the-Sun Party

Hint: Parents should accompany this age child so be sure to have plenty of lawn chairs and quilts for seating. Also a serve-yourself lemonade table works great.

Caution: Children should be supervised by parents at all times when playing near water or swimming.

Guest List: Ages 2 to 4 *and* their parents.

Invitations: Purchase inexpensive beach balls and write the party information on each ball with a permanent marker. Mail the deflated beach ball in a manila envelope or hand-deliver inflated beach ball invitation. Be sure to suggest proper dress: swim suits or play clothes. (See page 105.)

Favors: Neon sunglasses or visors, plastic shovel and bucket stuffed with tissue paper, bubbles, sidewalk chalk.

Food: Lemonade, sunshine cake and sunshine sherbet ice cream cones. In each glass of lemonade add a straw topped with a miniature paper parasol. Decorate round layer cake as a smiley sunshine cake.

Decorations: Dress two of the birthday child's favorite stuffed animals or dolls in bathing suits, sunglasses, and hats. Position them back to back in center of table. Attach helium-filled balloons to them to complete centerpiece.

FUN IN THE SUN!
WEAR YOUR BATHING SUIT!

Activities/Games:

(1) *Water Play:* Have several wading pools or yard sprinklers set up. As children arrive, they will make their own fun. Be sure to have water toys on hand such as wind-up toys, buckets, balls, boats and bubbles.

(2) *Sea Shell Treasure Hunt:* Hide small sea shells or toys in the sand. Use a sandbox, if available, or fill a small wading pool with sand. Cover until time for the game. Let children gather around and hunt for treasure.

(3) *Shaving Cream Finger Paint:* Place a large dollop of shaving cream in front of each child on formica top or glass top table. (Strongly caution the children about putting their hands in their mouths or eyes.) After children have made their designs, gently place a piece of blue or black construction paper on top. The shaving cream will stick. Turn the paper over and put it in a safe place to dry. Be sure each child's name is on his or her creation. Sponge or hose off tables for a quick clean up.

29

Sunshine Sherbet Ice Cream Cones:

Decorate ice cream cones filled with orange sherbet with a smiley face using decorator's icing and candy for features. Cones can be made the day ahead and stored in the freezer in muffin tins until just before serving.

Bubble Formula:

1 - 2   cups dishwashing liquid
6   cups water
3/4   cup white corn syrup (optional)

Mix. Let bubble formula settle for several hours before using. Pour into a 9x13x2-inch cake pan or pizza pan. Dip blower into bubble formula. (To avoid foaming, do not stir bubble formula with blower when dipping.)

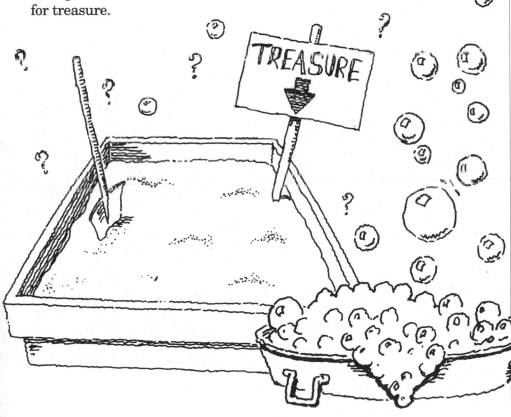

Old West Party

Celebrate Like the Olden' Days

Read some prairie stories to everyone from the collection of books by Laura Ingalls Wilder. Choose stories that talk about how people celebrated and had parties. *On the Banks of Plum Creek* and *Little House in the Big Woods* have wonderful stories that will delight children.

Guest List: Ages 2 to 6.

Invitations: Copy the lasso pattern provided (see page 106), add a photo of your child in western wear, and reproduce on copy machine. Be sure to ask children to come in jeans or western wear.

Favors: Western hats, bandannas, small packages of plastic figures and horses.

Food: Sheet cake decorated with western figures and horses. Have extra figures on hand, so each child is served a slice of cake with a figure or horse on top.

Decorations: Create a "WANTED" poster using your child's photo. Make copies and enlargements to be used as decorations. Start early collecting western items such as real horse shoes, cowboy boots and spurs, rope, and a wagon wheel. Use them as table decorations and props.

Activities/Games:

(1) *Personalized Sheriff Badges:* Before the party, cut construction paper badges, gather pencils, markers, glitter and glue. Supply each child with a personalized badge to decorate. Have helper supervise decorating. Place badge on each child with masking tape.

(2) *Arrange a Pony Ride:* Inquire at local riding stables, summer camps, or farms whether they arrange pony rides for kids. Be sure the stable is trained for novice riders. You'll need extra parents to help the kids while riding. If possible, find a stable with an indoor ring in case of rain.

(3) *Stick Horse Relay:* Decorate miniature brooms as stick horses using bandannas. Mark relay turnarounds using helium-filled balloons tied to real horseshoes.

(4) *Horseshoe or Ring Toss:* Use plastic horseshoes instead of real ones for safety's sake. Set targets about six to ten feet from throwing line. Players stand behind throwing line and toss rings or horseshoes in turn.

Howdy, Partner! Which way to GEORGIA'S Party?

Super Hero Party

You can substitute your child's favorite super hero or cartoon hero.

Comic Book Read-Aloud Time

Buy a couple of popular comic books. Gather everyone in a circle after presents are exchanged and read excerpts from the books to the kids as time allows.

Guest List: Ages 4 to 6.

Invitations: See page 107.

Favors: Greet children with their red hero capes and age-appropriate comic books.

Food: Sheet cake with super hero emblem or figures and punch color-coordinated with super hero. Current super hero cake pans are available at cake decorating supply stores.

Decorations: Use paper products in super hero colors of red, blue and yellow. For door decorations, draw poster of super hero, replacing hero's face with birthday child's photo. Change the name of the super hero to include your child's name.

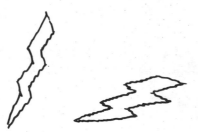

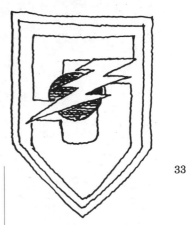

Activities/Games:

(1) *Modeling Clay Center:* Have green "kryptonite" play dough or modeling clay for beginning activity. Be sure to have rolling pins and cookie cutters on hand. Cover table with washable cloth.

(2) *Hot Potato Kryptonite:* Children sit in circle. Give one player the potato (that you have painted with green acrylic paint) to pass. A super hero sits in the center with hands over eyes. When hero says "Pass the Kryptonite," the green potato starts around the circle. When hero says, "HOT POTATO KRYPTONITE," whoever has the potato becomes "it" and trades places with the super hero in the center.

(3) *Super Hero Photo:* Have a poster-sized drawing of the super hero. Cut out face. Let each child hold poster with his face in the hole. Take instant snap shot for an additional favor.

(4) *Blast Off Super Fast Relay:* Form two teams and line up. First person in each line runs to designated spot, turns and runs back to tag next in line. First team to have all players run down and back is the winner.

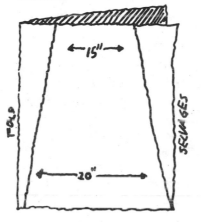

Super Hero Cape Pattern:

1. Fold 2/3 yard of fabric as shown with selvages together.
2. With soft lead pencil, draw cape shape as shown in diagram.
3. Cut neck edge using sewing shears and use pinking shears to cut bottom and sides of cape.
4. Bind the neck using 40 inches of double fold bias binding. Allow enough binding at each end to make ties. Knot ends. Makes 2 capes.

"I Made It Myself" Art Party

Creative Clay

1 cup cornstarch
1 cup baking soda
1 1/4 cups cold water
Mix ingredients together in a saucepan over medium heat, stirring constantly. Stir, about 5 minutes. Cool. Store in covered container.

Making Pinch Pots

1. Give each child a ball of clay the size of a large egg.
2. Demonstrate how to roll the clay into ball. Do not use newsprint to cover work area, as ink will dirty clay.
3. Using both thumbs, press down gently in center, turning the clay as you work to form bowl shape.
4. To form wider dish shape, pull out on sides of clay pot as you are pressing toward center. Keep turning as you work so that thickness of sides will be even.
5. Decorate outside of pot using toothpick.

Guest List: Ages 4 to 7. Ten to twelve children. Be sure to have adequate adult supervision.

Invitations: This is a great party for the birthday child to make his or her own invitation. Supply child with paper and black marker and let his or her creativity take over. Fill in party information and run off copies of drawing and allow child to color in invitation using colored markers. Request that each child bring a paint shirt to protect clothing.

Favors: Favors will be the art projects the children have made—edible necklaces, clay projects, and finger or pudding paintings. Make sure each completed project is labeled with the artist's name.

Food: Cupcakes or layered cake decorated as artist palette. Ice cake with white frosting, make palette outline using a dark-colored frosting. Add dollops of red, yellow, blue, green, purple and orange icing around palette.

Decorations: Collect art items: artist brushes, palette, tubes of paints, and beret to decorate table. Display a "Happy Birthday" poster on an easel to identify the party house.

Activities/Games:

Preparations: You will need three art stations covered in paper with adult supervision at each table.

(1) *Edible Jewelry:* As the children arrive, let them make edible jewelry. Before the party, cut colorful yarn twenty-four inches long. Tape one end of the yarn so children can thread the yarn through circle-shaped fruit cereal or circle candy holes to create bracelets or necklaces (24-inch shoelaces work great for stringing also).

(2) *Creative Clay:* Give each child a piece of clay. By example, show them how to make a simple animal or a pinch pot. Allow children to make something. Using a toothpick put child's initials on the bottom.

(3) *Finger Painting:* Instruct the children about finger painting and give each child a rectangle of freezer wrap paper, slick side up, and a dollop of one color paint. Watch the fun! Be sure to have a clean-up spot; this activity is messy, but the children adore it!

Pudding Painting: For very young children we recommend pudding painting instead of finger painting. Use individual containers of snack pudding and follow the directions given for finger painting except no water is necessary.

(4) *Decorate Cupcakes:* As the children clean up from finger painting, have helpers remove paper table coverings and place bowls of different colored icings, jelly beans, colored sprinkles, colorful candies, and plastic spreading knives on the tables. The children create edible masterpieces.

Finger Painting

1. Cover work area with thick pad of newspaper.
2. Give each child a large rectangle of freezer paper with slick/plastic side up.
3. Using squirt bottles filled with water, wet each child's paper.
4. Instruct children to spread water evenly over <u>entire</u> paper. Caution children that if paper becomes too dry it will tear. If paper is too wet, drain off some of the water.
5. Give each child a dollop of finger paint. Use fingertips, the side of hands, arms and even elbows. Be creative!
6. Check dryness of paper as children work. Reapply water and/or paint as necessary.
7. Hang finished art on clothesline, or leave on tables to dry.

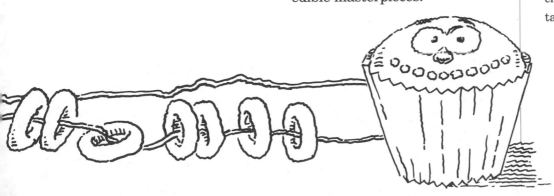

Low-Cost Party Favors

Party favors don't have to be expensive. In fact, the ones that kids treasure the most are those they make themselves at the party. If you buy favors, try to buy things that really can be used, like chalk or magnets.

- Baby food jar filled with candies, circle of colored tissue paper secured to top with curling ribbon.
- A single, blooming plant such as a marigold, petunia, or pansy planted in a small paper cup.
- Birdseed ornaments cut from bread with cookie cutters, dried in a slow oven, brushed with egg whites, sprinkled with birdseed, and hung on a tree with a pipe cleaner.
- Pie pan wind chimes assembled from odds and ends (keys, nails, jar lids, shells), tied with thread through holes punched around the pie pan, and hung from a twine loop through the center.
- Recipe holders made from clothespins decorated with nature's treasures (rocks, fossils, shells, seeds) or construction paper designs (animals, birds, butterflies).
- Necklaces fashioned from pieces of candy rolled in a piece of clear plastic wrap, tied with curling ribbon between each piece of candy, and a piece of ribbon connecting the two ends.

Favorite Favors:

magnets

stickers

erasers

stamps

tracing tools

balls

balloons (not for toddlers)

bubbles and blowers

pinwheels

yo-yos

magic tricks

card games

sunglasses

light sticks

silly strains

bendable figures

tops

gliders

string streamers in a can

water yo-yos

noise makers

sidewalk chalk

note pads

pencils

clothespin butterflies

pom-pom critters

wind-up water toys

instant photos of kids at party

PARTIES *for* 7- to 10-Year-Olds

Snow or Sand Sculpture Party

Plastic Scoop

As shown in the illustration, cut away the bottom corner of a 1/2 gallon plastic milk container (the kind with a handle) to make a scoop. The scoop may be used for making the sand or snow sculptures, or for playing catch with a tennis ball.

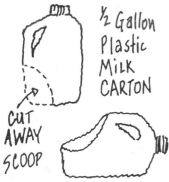

½ Gallon Plastic Milk Carton

CUT AWAY SCOOP

Pita Bread Sandwiches

1/2 cup mayonnaise
2 tablespoons mustard
3 oz. thinly sliced turkey
2 pita bread rounds
sweet or dill pickles, sliced
swiss cheese, shredded
lettuce leaves

Cut pita bread in half. Open to make pocket and fill.
Makes 4 sandwiches.

This party is a great yard party on a snowy day or beach party during warm weather. Be certain to tell guests to dress appropriately — dry socks for snow party and sunscreen and towel for beach party.

Guest List: Ages 7 and up.

Invitations: See page 108.

Favors: Homemade jug scoop made at party, or sand sculpture in jar. Kites are great favors for the beach. Photographs of the children and their sculptures.

Food: *Snow Party*: Hot chocolate or hot cider and a Snowman Cake made from a 9-inch and an 8-inch cake pan. *Beach Party*: Starfish cake (see illustration). For the beach, lots of cool things to drink including 3-gallon jug of water. Pita bread sandwiches and chips (see recipe).

Decorations: For an outdoor party, nature has already done a magnificent job of decorating.

Activities/Games:

(1) *Sand or Snow Sculpture:* Sculptures may be as simple as building a sand castle or snowman or as complex as creating animals, people, forts, or igloos. Children may work individually or in groups. Begin by brainstorming an idea. Then select a location and general layout. Provide buckets and small shovels or homemade scoops.

Sand or snow needs to be wet to be molded or packed. To mold: pack wet sand or snow into containers of different sizes and shapes, then invert and gently tap bottom of container and carefully remove mold. (A metal bread pan makes a great form for a snow brick.) To pack: pile wet sand or snow into the desired shape, pack gently using hands, then use shovels, scoops, shells, or spoons to carve details.

Take pictures of the children and their sculptures and give to the kids.

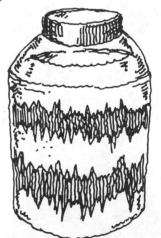

(2) *Layered Sand Sculpture in a Jar:* Divide sand into bowls, a bowl for each color. If sand is of poor quality, table salt is an excellent substitute. Mix enough powdered food coloring into sand to color. Provide each child with a small, clear plastic jar with lid (glass is not allowed on most public beaches). With a spoon or scoop, layer sand one color on top of another. As layers are placed, push length of 1/8-inch wooden dowel or a plastic knife down the inside walls of jar to make designs. Continue layering sand until jar is *completely* full. Replace lid when finished.

(3) *Feed the Wildlife Tree:* Children may learn to care for wildlife by decorating a tree with nuts, fruit, popcorn, and other edibles. With adult supervision, children enjoy hanging completed ornaments on a small tree.

Starfish Cake

Bake a two-layer round cake. Leave one layer whole and cut other into five equal sections as shown in illustration. Trim curved side of each section to fit snugly against remaining round layer. Attach to round cake with icing to make starfish as shown. Frost with yellow icing and shake on colored sprinkles while icing is still damp.

Wildlife Tree Ornaments

• String popcorn and berries with a needle and thread.
• Coat pine cones with peanut butter; roll in birdseed.
• Tie three pieces of millet (from pet store) together to form a triangle.
• Press sunflower seeds into an apple.
• Cut cookie cutter shapes from bread; dry in slow oven.
• Cut oranges in half; sprinkle with seeds.

Backyard Camping Party

Dogs-in-a-Blanket

Roll out one canned biscuit. Wrap around a hotdog. Moisten the edges of the dough and press them together to seal. Hotdog should be sticking out each end. Put on a stick and roast over hot coals or bake in oven at 350° for 15 to 20 minutes

Trail Snack

In a large container combine equal amounts of raisins, dry or honey-roasted peanuts, and candy-coated chocolate bits. To this mixture you may also add any of the following: dried apples, chopped dried apricots, coconut flakes, or sunflower seeds.

Have a plan in case of rain or if a child is homesick or scared of the dark. There should be a place where kids can come inside and sleep, if necessary. Also, be sure kids know where the bathroom is before bed-time. There should be one adult per tent.

Have one or two 3- or 4-person tents set up. If you don't have tents, either borrow them from neighbors, rent them, or make your own using a clothesline or fence. Each guest needs to bring a sleeping bag, pillow, PJ's, toothbrush and stuffed animal.

Guest List: Ages 7 to 10. Keep the party small.

Invitations: See page 108. Note to parents on invitation to pick up children at set time the next morning.

Favors: Light sticks, pen-lights, or flashlights given upon arrival to be used during the party.

Food: Dogs-in-a-blanket, trail snack (see recipe), and camper cake, plus milk, juice, or other caffeine-free drinks. Adult hosting party will need to provide breakfast.

Decorations: Nature has provided a canopy of stars and sound effects of the great outdoors.

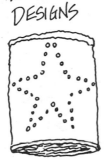

LANTERN DESIGNS

Activities/Games:

(1) *Tin Can Lanterns:* Before the day of the party, fill cans with water and freeze overnight. Cut strips of brown paper just to fit around the can. One can and one paper pattern per guest, plus a few extras. As soon as the children arrive have them draw a simple dot "lantern" design on brown paper pattern. Use masking tape to attach pattern to can. With adult supervision, children place can on folded towel, and using hammer and nail, hammer the dot design. Remove paper design; let ice melt. Set cans on table with flashlight or lighted votive candle inside.

(2) *Backyard Tent:* A tent can be made from almost any heavy material such as an old rug, or bedspread, or unbleached muslin. Hang over a fence, clothesline, or even a picnic table. Use a plastic drop cloth to cover the ground. Guests will play happily in their tents.

(3) *Endless Stories:* Gather children in the tent or on a blanket in a circle. Have birthday child begin a story. After a minute or two, have another child continue the story, until all have helped make up a very tall tale.

(4) *Star Gazing:* Before the party, adult makes a map of the night sky with Polaris (north star) in the center. This is painted on the underneath side of an old black umbrella using a white paint pen. Connect stars to show constellations. Use umbrella outdoors to help locate constellations by opening it and pointing its tip toward Polaris.

Camper Cake

Frost a two-layer rectangular cake with chocolate or brown-tinted icing. Using a leaf tube, frost inverted ice cream cones as trees, and let dry. To make camper, mound red icing for sleeping bag with a yellow zigzag for zipper; use a marshmallow for a pillow; and draw facial features and hair on a vanilla wafer using icing tips. For campfire, use pretzels for firewood, and add red and yellow icing for flames. Add plastic wildlife animals. Print birthday message, and add candles.

Time Capsule Party

Watermelon Surprise Capsule

1. Cut off the top third of a watermelon to make the lid. Scoop out watermelon. Remove seeds and cut melon into bite-size pieces.
2. Cut up other fruit such as cantaloupe, oranges, apples, strawberries, and grapes. Mix all fruit.
3. Fill watermelon capsule with mixed fruit and cover with lid.
4. Push birthday candles into top.

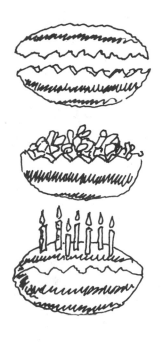

A time capsule is a sealed container holding objects that preserve a record of a particular time in history to be opened at some time in the future. Items of social and scientific interest, as well as objects of everyday life, are usually included such as photographs, small articles of clothing, letters, descriptions of current life, magazine clippings, perhaps a paper clip or postage stamp.

Cornerstones of buildings are sometimes hollowed out to hold time capsules. This continues a custom practiced in ancient Egypt and Babylon where small statues and inscriptions were sealed into temple foundations. Your guests will bring their capsules home to bury at least one foot deep and mark with a rock.

Guest List: Ages 7 to 10. Keep the party small.

Invitations: See page 109.

Favors: Each guest takes home his or her own time capsule. Host adult takes an instant photo of each child with friends to be included in time capsule.

Food: Watermelon Surprise Capsule.

Decorations: Before the party, make a brown paper tablecloth. Using glue, magazine pictures, newspaper articles, copies of illustrations from favorite short stories, and photos, have your child make a collage about the events in everyday life to glue to tablecloth. Make a mobile of "Things of Today," using pencils, favorite candy bar, stuffed animal, advertisements of favorite fast foods or fashions.

Activities/Games:

(1) *Time Capsules:* Children create their own capsules to bury in their backyards. Host parents provide capsules, which might be small, airtight plastic food containers or even old panty-hose eggs sealed with silicone caulking. Instruct children to bury their capsules at least one foot deep.

Provide scissors, paper, pens, magazines, old newspapers, candy wrappers, food labels, school menus, current movie listings, small everyday items such as a penny, barrette, paper clip for children to use in making their capsules. Children will need plenty of work space for this project.

Suggest that children include additional items from home to personalize their time capsules. Some items that might be included are snapshots of family, friends, and pets, ticket stubs from concerts, plays, or sporting events recently attended, current fad items, a coin, a popular toy, a baseball card, tape cassette of popular singing group or dated items.

(2) *Letters to the Future:* Children write letters to the future telling what life is like for them and how people celebrate birthdays.

(3) *Map:* Children draw maps of where they plan to bury their capsules at home. This is so they can find them again!

(4) *The Dragon's Tail:* Line children up, one in front of the other, with hands extended out onto the shoulders of the next child. The object of this non-competitive game is for the child at the beginning of the line to tag the child at the end of the line.

(5) *Gossip:* Adult makes up a short story and whispers it to first child seated in a circle. This child whispers it to the child to the right and so on until it is passed to each child. The last child repeats out loud the story and then the adult tells the original story.

Gone Fishin'

This party lends itself to two and a half hours and would work well along with a picnic or cookout. A good after-school party.

Caution: Children should be supervised by parents at all times when playing near water or swimming.

Boat Rides:

If you have access to a fishing boat, it is a special treat for one adult to take two children at a time around the lake in the boat. Of course, everyone wears a life jacket. The kids get a chance to row and try their luck fishing another spot. Limit the time to ensure that each child gets a turn in the boat.

Guest List: Ages 7 to 10. Keep this party small, no more than five or six. They must be old enough to operate a casting rod or bait their own hook. Otherwise, you need one helper for every two children.

Invitations: See page 109.

Favors: A photo of each child and his or her catch, fish to take home, or personalized tackle box are appropriate favors for this age.

Food: Apples, celery and carrot sticks, chips, dips, brownies, plenty of cold soft drinks and pick-up sandwiches or fried chicken.

Decorations: Use colorful paper goods.

Activities/Games:

Preparations: Check your area for a fish farm or other public fishing area. Collect items you will need for fishing such as sinkers, line, hooks, bobbers, pliers, work gloves, a few extra poles, landing net, stringer, a first aid kit. A small tackle box is useful in organizing this gear. Check on picnic table facilities.

(1) *Fish:* Helpers, preferably with some prior experience, will be needed to bait and remove fish from hooks, repair lines, and replace hooks. Let children know how much time they will have to fish.

(2) *Picnic:* Keep it simple.

(3) *Fish Not Biting?:* Some children may loose patience with fishing, especially if the fish aren't biting. Plan some alternate activities where children can come and go. For example, have softballs, soccer balls and toss toys available. Water games are fun if this is an option at your location. Be aware of other people fishing, the area where the children may play, and the possibility of balls going into the lake. With sports equipment on hand and some suggestions from you, like teaching them to skip rocks, children will make their own fun.

Awards:

Before the party day, purchase inexpensive trophies from an awards or party supply shop. Name of award can be applied using gummed labels. Be sure to bring a few with no award name because the children will come up with their own ideas. Suggested awards:

Largest fish,
Smallest fish,
Ugliest fish,
Most caught,
No catch.

Ball Cake:

Decorate the cake with blue icing; then add candy worms, fish, and bugs.

Bake Your Own Cake

Try to provide healthy snacks and drinks for kids along with sweets (see page 82 for ideas).

Guest List: Ages 7 to 9. Invite a small group of five to six children depending on the number of helpers available and the size of your kitchen. You will need one helper for every three children.

Invitations: Write the party information on a recipe card. (See page 110.)

Favors: Cookie cutter tied to a personalized wooden spoon. Simple aprons could be cut out of vinyl or plastic-coated fabric with twill tape sewn for ties. Children take home their decorated cake.

Food: Cake and ice cream.

Decorations: Turn your front door into a pastry shop window. Using butcher paper and paint, create _(birthday child's name)_ Bake Shop with trays of scrumptious treats displayed on several shelves. Make sure parent of birthday child wears a chef's hat and apron. A banner inside could read Chef _(birthday child's name)_ Kitchen. As table decorations, use miniature measuring spoons, rolling pins, cookie cutters, sifters, and wooden spoons.

Activities/Games:

(1) *Create a Tablecloth:* Have table covered with freezer paper, slick side down. Children color with markers until all guests arrive.

(2) *Bake Your Own Cake:*

A. Set up one tray per person. On each child's tray have everything needed for preparing the cake. Use individually boxed microwave cakes, one box per child.

B. Prepare a set-up for yourself so you can demonstrate step-by-step the cake making process.

C. You need a helper to bake cakes and clean up while you move with the children to another area. Allow 5 minutes cooking time for each cake in the microwave.

(3) *Refreshments and Gift Opening:* Serve guests traditional birthday cake and open presents while mini-cakes bake.

(4) *Egg and Spoon Relay:* Divide children in two groups. Each relay team has a metal tablespoon and a hard-boiled egg. Hold the spoon at the end of the handle and use only one hand. In turn, each team member carries the egg in the spoon to a given point, then returns and hands the spoon to the next child in line. The team that finishes first wins.

(5) *Balloon Hop:* Divide children into two teams. First child on each team places an inflated balloon between his or her knees. At the signal, children hop to turn around spot, remove balloon and run back to starting line, and hand balloon to next in line. If balloon pops, an adult supplies another balloon. If a child drops the balloon, it is replaced between the knees before continuing. The first team to finish wins.

(6) *Cake Decorating:* Have kitchen helper reset table with decorating items including icing, gum drops, sprinkles, colorful candies, and plastic spreading knives. Children decorate their own cake and take it home as their favor.

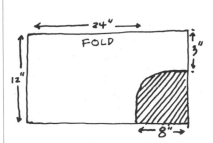

Apron Pattern:

1. Draw apron pattern in the shape as shown in diagram on folded brown paper. Cut out the part that is shaded.
2. Use 2/3 yard of vinyl or plastic-coated fabric. Position paper pattern on fabric, pin and cut.
3. Sew on 1/2-inch-wide twill tape for ties as shown.

WRITE CHILD'S NAME WITH PAINT PENS

Pen Pal Party

International Pen Pals

If you would like a pen pal from another country, there are organizations that specialize in matching people up. Look for pen pal service listings at your local library. When you contact the organizations:

1. Make sure names are exchanged—one to one—not lists of names sent out.
2. Include the ages, sex, hobbies, and general interests of the children.
3. Include a self-addressed, stamped envelope.
4. Ask how much they charge. Some pen pal services charge from three to five dollars to match individuals; others have no charge.

Having pen pals is a great way to make friends. Children can learn about their differences and similarities with children in other areas. One of the best things about having a pen pal is getting lots of letters!

Guest List: Ages 7 to 10.

Invitations: Drawing of two children holding hands on the front (colored by host child). For another idea, see page 114.

Favors: Colored pens, pencils, markers tied with curling ribbon.

Food: Baked potatoes, fruit salad, soft drinks. Suggested toppings for potatoes: bacon, sour cream, butter, chives, cheese, ham cubes, salt and pepper. Children love preparing their own potatoes. Serve frosted gingerbread cookies shaped like boys and girls. If you would prefer a cake, frost a round two-layer cake and attach frosted gingerbread cookie children around the sides of the cake.

Decorations: Balloons and banners in front of house and inside.

Activities/Games:

(1) *Pick-a-Pal:* Well in advance of the party, the host adult obtains a list of children who would like to be pen pals with the party guests. The list might come from a school or church or synagogue in a nearby community, another state, or even in another country (in planning, consider the additional expense and inconvenience of international mail). Put the names and addresses on slips of paper. Each party guest picks one of the names out of a hat to be his or her pen pal.

(2) *Thumbprint Stationery:* Using an ink pad, have children make several finger prints on plain stationery-size paper. Using colored pencils or pens, draw wings, facial features, arms, legs, tails to create animals and insects.

(3) *Pen Pal Letter:* Children write letters to pen pals and mail them. Take pictures of each child and enclose them with letters.

(4) *Balloon Pop Relay:* Divide children into teams. Give each child a balloon. At the signal, the first team member runs to a chair, sits on the balloon to pop it and returns to starting point. The other players follow. The first team to finish wins. Store pre-blown balloons in garbage bag. Pick up all balloon scraps immediately in households with toddlers.

Movie Night

Guest List: Ages 7 and up.

Invitations: Make your own out of construction paper to resemble a theater ticket. Length of party depends on the length of movie. (See page 110.)

Favors: Play money given to children as they arrive.

Food: Concession stand foods: popcorn, pizza, soft drinks.

Decorations: Concession stand poster. Check local video stores for promotional movie displays to decorate party room.

Activities/Games:

(1) *Flashlight Tag:* This is a good game to play while waiting for all guests to arrive. Add new players to the game as they arrive. Played outside on the lawn if boundaries are safe and game is well supervised. One player is "it." Armed with a flashlight, "it" searches for the other players and tries to "tag" one of them with the beam of the flashlight. When another player is "tagged," he becomes "it." Somewhere in the playing field there is a safe home base, such as a tree or bench, where players can rest without being "tagged." Allow children to use home only twice per game.

(2) *Movie Admission:* Have children bring invitation (ticket) to be admitted to your home. You may need to have extras in case some forget. Set up table at entrance. An older sibling could be the ticket taker, dressed in white shirt, black pants, and black bow tie.

(3) *Concession Stand:* After all have arrived, have children go to "concession stand" — banners over kitchen door show the way. Have poster with foods available and their prices. Children order and pay for food with play money.

(4) *Show Time!:* Proceed to movie room. Have chairs set up so all can see. Be prepared for spills. Start video. Please consider and preview what you show young people!

Homemade Pizza
Have the kids make their own homemade pizzas using store-bought dough. Put out tomato sauce, shredded mozzarella, sliced mushrooms, sliced peppers, sliced onions, sliced pepperoni, sliced olives, and other toppings. Cook at 450° for 10-15 minutes.

Backwards Party

Girls with long hair can wear their hair in a front ponytail sticking through the opening of a baseball cap worn backwards.

Guest List: Ages 7 to 10.

Invitations: Print invitation backwards, hold to a mirror to read. Instruct children to wear clothes backwards. (See page 111.)

Favors: Cups with names painted backwards filled with candy, twisted straws and other items such as silly putty or super string.

Food: Hot dogs or "pigs-in-a-blanket," juice or punch in baby bottles with nipples, cake and ice cream. Serve everything backwards; serve hot dog supper after guests have had cake and ice cream. Use relighting candles and sing "Happy Birthday" after cake has been eaten.

Decorations: Make a birthday banner to hang outside; of course, spell the words backwards! Set table backwards, cups and plates upside down, forks and spoons reversed and upside down.

Activities/Games:

(1) *"Hello," "Good-bye":* As guests arrive at front door, greet them with "good-bye" and instruct them to walk backwards to the back door.

(2) *Backwards Modeling:* After everyone arrives, have children walk backwards and model outfits. A prize could be given for the child wearing the most items backwards.

(3) *Three-Legged Race:* Play this with partners or team relay. Children pair off. Tie one child's right leg to another child's right leg (have one child face backwards). Each pair should be allowed a few minutes practice moving as a unit. At the signal, they make their way to the turning line and back again. The first team to complete the course wins.

(4) *Backwards Egg and Spoon Relay:* Play the relay backwards. (See instructions on page 47.)

(5) *Crab Relay:* Divide into teams. First child in line sits on floor with back toward finish line. When the whistle blows, the child walks backwards on hands and feet lifting hips off the ground. When the child reaches the other end of the room, he or she stands up, runs back, and touches the next player who takes a turn. The first team to finish wins.

Pigs-in-a-Blanket:

Preheat oven to 375°. Separate refrigerator crescent roll dough into triangles. Slit a hot dog lengthwise and fill with chunks of cheddar cheese. Place dog along short side of triangle and roll up in dough. Can be prepared ahead of time and refrigerated until time to pop into the oven. Bake 12 to 18 minutes until golden brown. Serve immediately.

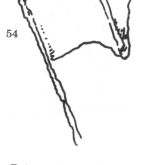

Baseball Game Party

Bring water and oranges cut in quarters to the game. Have a first aid kit on hand for minor bumps and bruises. For younger kids, use a softball rather than a hardball—or a whiffle ball for a backyard game. Be flexible. If your child is into soccer or basketball, change the party accordingly.

Guest List: Ages 7 to 10 (enough for two teams).

Invitations: A great outside party at a local baseball field. Have a rain date or plan. (See page 111.)

Favors: Baseball cards, gum, team caps or pins, posters of players, baseball magazines.

Food: Sheet cake decorated as a baseball field. Plastic baseball players and pennants available at grocery stores in the bakery department can be added to cake. Candles may be placed on each base and in outfield positions.

Decorations: Decorate inflated white helium balloons with black marker to resemble baseballs. Use these to identify party location.

COME TO MY BIRTHDAY PARTY

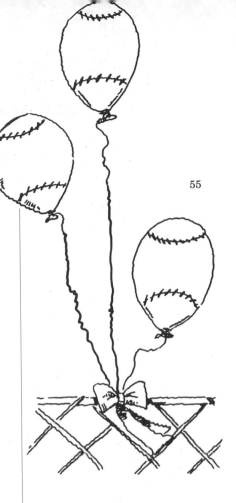

Activities/Games:

(1) *Baseball:* Be sure to clear using the field with baseball commissioner. Play a three-inning baseball game. Children could draw for positions. Have a poster board with drawing of field. As each child draws a position (written on sticky-backed paper), place it on poster board. You could redraw for positions for each inning; however, this may be too confusing for younger children. If this is done, be sure to have extra boxes with positions written out for children to draw from. Also assign batting order. Parent or older experienced teen would be a good pitcher; young children could use a T-ball set-up for batting. For older children, secure a qualified umpire.

(2) *Musical Present:* This could be played if you need a game after guests have finished refreshments and opened gifts. Wrap a gift. Then wrap it again in larger box. Wrap a third time in larger box. Have children sit in circle. Start music from cassette. Have players pass gift, one to another. When music stops, the person holding the gift unwraps it. If it is still wrapped, the person must pass it on when music starts again. Continue until the gift has been unwrapped completely. That person gets to keep gift.

"Gotcha" Party

Guessing Games

Play a guessing game after the cake and presents. Charades is a fun game that everyone can enjoy. Write down 10 easy words that all the children will know. Have one child stand before the others and imitate one of the words without talking. The others try to guess the word. The person who guesses correctly takes a turn at imitating the next word. Be sure everyone gets a turn.

Surprise your guests for dinner.

Guest List: Ages 8 and up.

Invitations: Phone parents to invite guests. Carefully explain time, date, procedure and emphasize that you want their child to be surprised. Also indicate if you will bring children home after dinner or where and when parents should pick them up.

Favors: Instant photo of guest being "got."

Food: Limit menu choices to 2 or 3 items to avoid confusion. Cake and ice cream.

Decorations: Birthday child and siblings decorate car with banner and balloons.

Activities/Games:

(1) *"Gotcha":* Arrive at each child's home, ring the doorbell and cajole, pick up, or bodily carry the laughing guest from the house. Birthday parent needs to be ready with camera to take pictures as the fun builds. Be sure to capture an instant photo of each child's "gotcha" to be put on a poster at the party, then given to the guest as a favor. *Do not reveal to the guests where you are taking them.*

(2) *Dinner:* Take a picnic to a favorite city park or state park. Ask a few parents along to help supervise. Pack blankets and a simple lunch of sandwiches, colas and juice, fruit, and a birthday cake. Be sure there's extra food for seconds.

(3) *Free Play:* Take a large rubber ball to the park with you. The kids can play any number of games, including dodgeball and kickball, before or after the picnic.

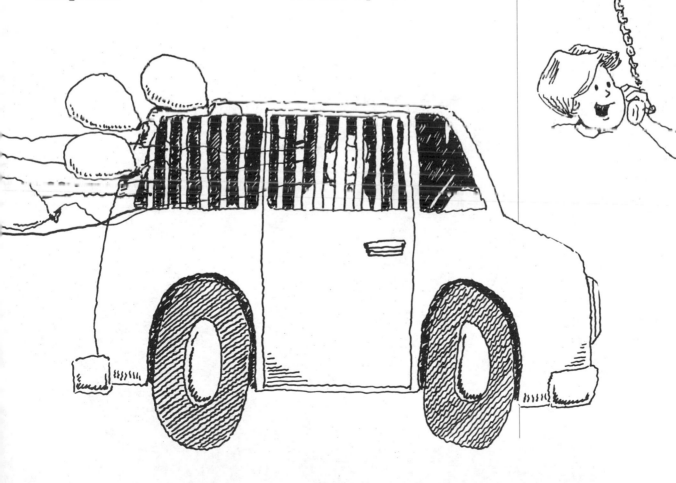

Sock Hop

Paw Print Socks

Pair of white, cotton socks
Cardboard strip
Scrap paper
No. 1 pencil
Fabric paint and
  paintbrush

Practice sketching
paw prints
on paper.

Stretch a sock
over cardboard
strip. Use the
pencil to outline
a paw print on the
sock bottom. Fill in
the print with the paint.
Repeat with other sock.
Let dry.

Ask that each child come
dressed as a song. Then
after everyone arrives,
have the others guess
what song each person is
dressed as.

Guest List: Ages 8 and up.

Invitations: See page 112.

Favors: Neon-colored socks
or Paw Print Socks.

Food: Cake and plenty to
drink! Ice round layer cake to
resemble a record, or sheet
cake as a jukebox.

Decorations: Crepe paper
streamers and balloons. 45
RPM records on the tables.
Check local radio station for
promotional items such as
pencils and bumper stickers, to
use in decorating.

Activities/Games:

(1) *Sock Exchange:* Meet guests at the door where they exchange their shoes for neon-colored socks or Paw Print Socks.

(2) *Boogie-Woogie:* A young enthusiastic dancer or an aerobics teacher would be a good instructor. The instructor teaches several dances such as the twist, limbo, bunny hop, chain dances. Music: a mix of current popular tunes and some from the 1950s is great.

(3) *Refreshments and Opening Presents:* Make food available at the beginning of the party and plan to have gifts before the dancing gets started or at the end of the party.

(4) *More Dancing:* Children may free dance until parents arrive.

Play "Name That Tune" using a tape or CD player, or have a game of musical charades with guests imitating the names of songs without using their voices.

Come as You Are: A Breakfast Surprise

Lemon Pancake

1/2 cup flour
2 eggs
1/2 cup milk
Pinch nutmeg
1 teaspoon grated lemon
    zest
3/4 stick butter

Mix flour, eggs, milk, nutmeg, and lemon zest in a bowl. Melt all the butter in a 10-inch skillet on top of stove. Pour in the batter. Bake at 425° for 15-20 minutes in the oven. Sprinkle with confectioners' sugar or drizzle with maple syrup. Serves 4.

Guest List: Ages 8 to 10, great for teens, too. Consider transportation limitations when inviting guests.

Invitations: Phone parents of guests several days in advance, emphasize that children are to be surprised. Set time of party early enough so that most children will still be sleeping. Give parent approximate time you will be arriving for pick up and ending time of party. Party should be one and a half to two hours, including travel time.

Favors: Toothbrushes. Grab bag of surprises or make your own surprise ball.

Food: Lemon pancake, juice, milk, scrambled eggs, bacon, sausage.

Instead of the birthday cake, serve a large lemon pancake or french toast.

Decorations: Have your child make a sign to decorate car or van the day before party. Tie balloons to door handles.

Activities/Games:

(1) *Guest Round-Up:* Upon arrival at each house, you are led to the sleeping guest where everyone yells, "Surprise!" Guests will have varied reactions upon being awakened. The fun builds with the addition of each guest awakening the next. After all guests have been rounded up, everyone goes back to your home for breakfast and games.

(2) *Surprise Bag:* Write one letter on the front of each brown paper sack spelling the word S-U-R-P-R-I-S-E. Place one object that begins with that letter in the appropriate sack. Tie loosely with ribbons. Line up sacks so that they spell SURPRISE. Give each child a card with the word "surprise" printed vertically. Child will write down what he thinks is in each bag after he has felt the bag.

(3) *Surprise Ball:* Start with a small trinket such as a whistle or piece of candy. Wrap with crepe paper and continue to add small trinkets as you wrap until you get a baseball shape. Different colored crepe paper makes the balls more exciting. Tape the ends. Suggestions for trinkets: plastic rings, erasers, stickers, candy, small magic tricks, and balloons.

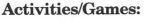

SURPRISE!

With the guests in pajamas, gather everyone outside for aerobics on the lawn.

Soccer Party

Football Goal Post

For a football party, turn your yard into a football field. Using nails, string, and white spray paint, create yard lines and end zones. Make goal posts out of wood or PVC pipe wrapped in crepe paper.

Guest List: Ages 8 to 11.

Invitations: See page 112.

Favors: Fun items with soccer ball motif such as stickers, pencil sharpeners, stationery, erasers.

Food: Set up card table for refreshments and gifts. Children may sit on ground or on bleachers. Hot dogs may be precooked, placed in buns, wrapped in foil, and kept warm in coolers. Serve popcorn in concession stand boxes or bags. Ice a sheet cake green and decorate as a soccer field with soccer ball in the center. With a toothpick, mark soccer ball on cake. Use brown icing for outline. Fill in sections of ball with brown and white icing. Write birthday message and add candles.

Decorations: Make a large birthday banner. Use pom-poms and pennants in school colors to help carry out the soccer theme. Stuff a soccer shoe with colored tissue paper. Secure helium-filled balloons to shoe.

Activities/Games:

Preparation: You need adults or teenage helpers to be coaches. Make arrangements to use a soccer field and borrow a net.

(1) *Goal Kick:* As children arrive, they line up on the field in front of goal. Determine distance from goal considering children's ages and goal size. Children take turns trying to kick the ball into the goal. An adult or older child could be the goalie. Goalie returns the ball to the next child.

(2) *Dribble Drill:* Set up sand-filled coffee cans or plastic cones slalom-style, with the first can 20 yards from the starting line and three additional cans about 10 feet apart. Dribbler must follow a course that zigzags from the right of one can to the left of the next, and so on. This game may also be played as a relay.

(3) *Free Play:* After food has been served and gifts have been opened, children play until parents arrive. Have several balls available.

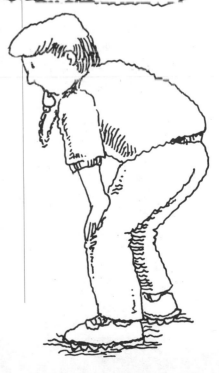

Breakfast and Baseball Card Show

Prepare plenty of food; kids this age eat a great deal.

Toad-in-the-Hole

1 1/2 tablespoons butter or margarine

2 thick slices bread, with a 2" hole cut out of each center

2 eggs

1/2 jar spaghetti sauce

2 thick slices cheese, mozzarella or provolone

1. Melt margarine in a large skillet on medium heat. Add bread. Brown for 2 to 3 minutes.
2. Crack eggs and drop into the centers of the bread slices. Cook for one minute, then flip and brown other side.
3. Pour spaghetti sauce over bread and cook until egg is cooked as desired.
4. Put cheese on top of bread and cover. Turn off heat. Serve when melted. Serves 2.

If you've never been to one, a baseball card show is usually held in a flea market setting. Dealers come from several states with booths to sell or trade baseball cards and paraphernalia. Often as a promotional attraction, a professional baseball player will be on hand to sign autographs.

Guest List: Ages 8 to 12. Limit number of guests.

Invitations: Include pick-up place and time on the invitation or state that you will bring the child home at a certain time. Have guests bring spending money and cards to trade or sell among each other or at the show. This is a 2 1/2- to 3-hour party. (See page 113.)

Favors: Big League Chew, baseball cards, pennants, baseballs.

Food: Bacon, eggs, sausage, biscuits, bagels, milk, juice, fruit.

Decorations: Use baseball posters, pennants, and crepe paper to decorate party room. For a fun morning get-together, no decorations are necessary.

Activities/Games:

(1) *Flick a Card:* Stand about 10 feet back from a wall. Two children take turns flicking cards out at the wall. When a card lands on another, wrong side up, that child picks up both cards. First card that lands on another, right side up, that child picks up all cards on the floor. Then, play again or with new challenger. Best played with old cards or duplicates.

(2) *Baseball Card Show:* Parental supervision is a must. Hand out tickets and go over your rules for the show, such as, stay with a partner and check in with parent every thirty minutes at a prearranged spot.

Pirate Scavenger Hunt

Guest List: Ages 8 and up.

Invitations: See page 113.

Favors: Bandannas, eye patches, or kaleidoscopes.

Collect items in advance for parties. During holidays, collect props and decorative objects in craft, party, or department stores. Watch for promotions in toy stores—even theme parks have loads of items to collect for later.

Food: Birthday cake with pirate theme and ice cream. Decorate a sheet cake using miniature, plastic pirate figures. Children may also enjoy the gold coins filled with chocolate on the table.

Decorations: Start collecting as much "junk jewelry" as you can find. Mardi Gras beads work great. Look for something that would work as a small treasure chest, a jewelry box perhaps. Gold chocolate coins and fish nets add to the pirate theme. Use a black tablecloth and gold or yellow paper plates. For the centerpiece, have your small treasure chest overflowing with jewels and gold coins. Scatter more jewelry and gold coins over the table.

AHOY MATES!!!
IT'S _Joel_'s BIRTHDAY!

Activities/Games:

(1) *Pirate Disguise:* As the children arrive, have your helpers put mustaches, bandannas and eye patches on the children.

(2) *Pirate Scavenger Hunt:* Call neighbors and inform them of the time that they may be visited by pirates. Prepare a list of items to be hunted and have a copy for each team. Recruit one teenage helper for every five children invited. Inform them of their responsibilities and be sure to have a bandanna and eye patch for each helper.

Divide the children into teams, each led by one helper. Set a time limit and boundary limits. Give each team its list and gold shopping bag for collected items and explain the rules (no more than two items at one house; give one point per item unless otherwise marked). The winning team is the team back on time with the most items. Send the teams out in different directions.

Be ready for excited, loud children to return. Check items and determine the winning team.

PIRATE PARTY
SCAVENGER HUNT LIST

a jelly bean
a toy boat
a cork
a map
a shoe string
a feather
a marble
a canceled stamp
a gold or silver paper-wrapped
        candy
a white hair
a cookie
a straw
a penny dated in the sixties
last Sunday's comics
a shoe box
a ponytail holder
a toothpick
a tooth
a Lego
a Pittsburgh Pirates baseball card
        (2 points)
a gold leaf
a gold or silver button
a picture of a pirate
a bone or skeleton
a tennis ball

Hint: The younger the children, the smaller the groups.

Sleep-Over Party

Wide-Awake Cake

1. On 3 vanilla wafers, draw facial features and hair using icing tips; let dry.

2. Ice top third of a 2-layer 9-inch cake with white icing. Mound icing for body shapes on lower 2/3 cake.

3. Position graham crackers for foot and headboards. Add marshmallow pillows, vanilla wafer heads and a graham cracker teddy bear with more icing.

4. Using star icing tip, cover lower 2/3 of cake with design to resemble a comforter.

5. Add edging around bottom of cake using a ruffle icing tip.

6. Attach stick candy for bed posts.

Tell Some Ghost Stories:

In the evening, turn lights out and light a couple of candles to set the mood for reading ghost stories. Have everyone get under blankets and settle in for a spooky tale.

Guest List: Ages 7 to 10. (Limit the number.)

Invitation: See page 114.

Favor: T-shirts, jewelry, hair brush, decorated at the party.

Food: White sheet cake decorated like the invitation with moon and stars or the Wide-Awake Cake. Supper: pizza, chips and dip, fruit. Breakfast: cereal, juice, milk. Keep it simple.

Decorations: Use crepe paper streamers and balloons to decorate party room.

Activities/Games:

(1) *Great Beginnings:* As the kids arrive, open gifts and eat supper. Then go to an outdoor activity such as badminton, croquet or putt-putt golf. Save birthday cake and crafts for later that evening.

(2) *Paint a T-Shirt:* Line inside of shirts with cardboard or wax paper to prevent paint from bleeding to shirt back. Use sponges dipped in fabric paint to decorate shirts. Let dry and heat-set painted shirts in the dryer.

(3) *Make Homemade Popcorn:* This is lots of fun, but parents will need to supervise. Place 1/4 cup oil in the bottom of a tall pot. Pour in 1 cup of unpopped corn and stir around to coat with oil. Heat on medium; cover and wait to hear popping as the oil heats the kernels. When popping stops, remove from heat and serve in bowls.

Provide a bag of dress up clothes. Children produce a skit for parent to video. Children watch video while enjoying refreshments.

More Party Games

You can never have enough games planned for a party. Sometimes a game is such fun the kids want to play it over and over. Other times you can run through your entire repertoire in 20 minutes flat! There doesn't need to be a prize for winners—the general party favors are plenty. In fact, some of the noncompetitive games suggested here are the most fun of all!

• **Skin the Snake**: Line up single file. Each child stoops over and places his right hand between his legs and with his left hand grasps the right hand of the player in front of him. When all are ready, the last player in line lies down on his or her back, while the line straddles and moves back over him or her. The next player then lies down and one by one the entire line does this until everyone is lying down. The last person to lie down, then stands up and walks forward, each following, until all are in standing position still holding hands. Congratulations, you have just skinned the snake!

• **Water Brigade**: Provide each team with two buckets (one empty and the other half-full of water). Place the full bucket at goal line. The first player runs to the goal line carrying the empty bucket, pours the water from the filled bucket into the empty bucket, leaves the empty bucket, and carries the filled bucket back to his team. The next player carries the filled bucket, transfers the water, and returns with the empty bucket. Continue until all have had a turn.

• **Wheelbarrow Relay**: One child in each pair walks on hands while the other child holds the feet as they race to a goal line and return.

• **Dizzy Izzy**: First player in line firmly places the end of a baseball bat on the ground. With his or her forehead on the bat, the player circles the bat. After seven circles, the player drops the bat and walks, runs, or crawls to the finish line, and makes way for the next player.

• **Egg or Water Balloon Toss:** Form two lines of players about 8 feet apart. Spread out the players to double arm's length, moving one line down to offset players so that the two lines are not facing directly across but diagonally between opposite players. Players gently toss raw eggs or water balloons back and forth diagonally from one player across to a player in the other line. See how many eggs or water balloons get to the end of the line.

• **Hula Hoop Pass**: Hold hands and stand an arm's length apart in a line or a circle. While holding hands step completely through the hula hoop and pass it from one player to the next without letting go of hands, until the hula hoop reaches the end of the line or completes the circle.

• **Sack Race**: First person in line puts both feet in a feed sack and hops to the goal line, hops back, gets out of the sack and gives it to the next person in line until everyone has had a turn.

• **Collective Blanket Ball**: Spread each team around a blanket. Everyone holds an edge. Place ball in the middle of one blanket. Toss the ball between blankets. Toss it over to the other team, or toss it straight up and move so the other team can move to your place and catch the ball before it hits the ground.

PARTIES *for* Preteens

Who's Too Old?

Many parents claim their children are "too old" for birthday parties when the kids reach their 10th birthday. The truth is that most preteens still enjoy getting together, but the emphasis should be more on getting together and having fun, and less on celebrating birthdays. With older ages, sometimes skipping the gifts means less embarrassment.

We have suggested some parties on the following pages that children this age and up really enjoy. Be creative. With planning and creativity, the party will be a hit for your child, his or her friends, and you.

Get Acquainted, Back-to-School Party

Preparation Hints:
Parents meet one month before end-of-summer party and volunteer for various jobs:

1. invitations, mailing—get list from school;
2. art and game supplies;
3. desserts;
4. beverages;
5. baskets, quilts, bandannas;
6. condiments, pickles, chips;
7. sandwiches;
8. activities.

The kid hosts should meet one month before party to address and mail the invitations. Hosts arrive at party one hour early to assemble food baskets.

This party requires several helpers depending on the number of guests.

Guest List: Ages 11 to 14 (30-75 people).

Invitations: Printed with school colors. (See page 115.)

Favors: Decorated notebooks, pencils printed with school name.

Food: Mushroom baskets lined with red and navy bandannas or bandannas of school colors. Basket menu: 1/2 turkey and 1/2 ham sandwich, condiments, dill pickles, brownies, petit fours, individual bags of potato chips. Canned soft drinks iced down in coolers nearby.

Decorations: Ribbons and balloons in school colors on a lamp post. A grapevine wreath decorated with apples and ribbons for the front door. Quilts, pennants, baskets lined with bandannas all add to the festive mood.

Activities/Games:

(1) *Who Can Say "Yes?"*:
Using red construction paper, cut out a large apple shape. Type a list of questions onto white paper. Cut it into an apple shape (slightly smaller than the red one) and staple it onto the red paper apple.

As the guests arrive, give each of them a sharpened red pencil and a "Yes" List. Kids search for someone who can say "yes" to each question and has person sign name. This allows time for everyone to arrive and for the guests to mingle. Wrap up the ice-breaker by reading aloud some of the questions and identifying those who answer "yes."

(2) *Sing For Your Supper:*
From a hat, the guests draw a piece of colored paper on which is written one verse or chorus of a song. On signal, after all have drawn, the guests sing the verse on their slips of paper. They are to find someone who is singing the other part of their song. This person is their supper partner.

Example:
(A) *Row, Row, Row, Your Boat Gently Down the Stream.*
(B) *Merrily, Merrily, Merrily, Merrily, Life Is but a Dream.*

After finding partners and picking up a basket supper, kids go outside to sit on quilts marked with colored pennants. Each teen locates the pennant with the same color as the paper that they have drawn from the hat. Assign groups of four to six to each quilt. In doing this, each guest shares supper with a new friend and has two to four more new friends to sit with at supper.

Find someone who can say "YES" to a question and have that person sign his or her name (a different person for each question).

1. Did you go to *(name of beach)* this summer?
2. Have you lived in *(city in another state)* ?
3. Do you take gymnastics?
4. Are you wearing black sneakers?
5. Did you go to *(popular camp)* this summer?
6. Do you want to be on the track team this year?
7. Do you play a string instrument?
8. Have you been up in a hot air balloon?
9. Do you hope to be on the basketball team?
10. Have you seen *(current movie)* ?
11. Do you have green eyes?
12. Do you have a pet bird?
13. Have you been white water rafting?
14. Are there four or more children in your family?
15. Are you an only child?
16. Have you been to *(another popular camp)* ?
17. Do you like to play tennis?
18. Do you have red hair?
19. Have you been to *(big city)* this summer?
20. Have you climbed a mountain?

Spaghetti under the Stars

If your children shy from the idea of a birthday celebration saying they're either too old or too cool for such parties—don't worry. Often getting friends together in a less "organized way" works better for preteens. Always let them help organize the get-together or party.

Guest List: Ages 11 and up. An outside dinner party for 12 or more, if adequate seating is available.

Invitations: Can be printed on 3" x 5" card and attached to plastic silverware, rolled in red napkin, tied with string or ribbon. Invitations can be hand-delivered. (See page 115.)

Favors: Place coupons to local frozen yogurt shop in balloons before they are blown up with helium. Use these balloons to decorate tables. Each guest receives one for a favor.

Food: Serve courses as in a restaurant. Take orders for soft drinks, then serve salads and remove bowls when finished. Serve main course of spaghetti with French bread. Waiters bring the birthday cake lit with sparkle candles to the table. Sing "Happy Birthday" to the honoree. Special cake sparklers available from a cake decorating supply store work great!

Decorations: Hang a BUON COMPLEANNO banner outside (Happy Birthday in Italian). Decorate the "restaurant" scene with red and white-checked tablecloths. Use black lanterns as center-pieces with green, red and white helium balloons tied to them. Italian flags and other decor could be borrowed from an Italian restaurant.

Spaghetti under the Stars

Celebrating

Loris' Birthday!

Activities/Games:

Italian Dinner: Use older high
school kids for waiters, experienced waiters preferable.
Have them dress alike in black
pants and white shirts with
bow ties.

Hint: Music is essential.
If a strolling accordion
player can't be found,
play Italian songs for
background music.

Pre-Theater Dinner

Consider having a dinner party before other events: sports, school, community or church. You supply dinner and an open home for your teen and friends, while the event itself serves as after-dinner entertainment. Teenagers enjoy gathering for eating, but are eager to get on their way to the event. The result is a fun, short party during which you have an opportunity to make teens feel welcome in your home as well as get to know them better.

Use ideas from the setting of the play to establish a theme. For instance, if your guests will be attending *The King and I*, create an oriental setting: decorate with paper lanterns and streamers, serve an oriental dinner on low tables with pillows to sit on, provide chopsticks, and finish off with dessert embellished with a paper umbrella and fortune cookies on the side.

Guest List: Ages 11 to 17.

Invitations: Relate invitations to the theme of a local musical or play. (See page 116.)

Favors: Relate your favors to the theme of the party. If you find the theme a challenge, then create homemade admission tickets to give to the children to use as a "meal ticket."

Food: For cultural themes, create a menu that reflects the region represented in the musical or play. In many cases, it won't be as easy to reflect your theme in the food you serve. Most any menu will work: build-your-own-sandwiches, potato chips, fruit, soda and juice.

Decorations: To transform the party room into a restaurant scene, hang colored beads or crepe paper streamers in the doorway. Use two long tables decorated with paper tablecloths. Use your imagination in decorating. Often, you'll find many items that will relate to the theme right in your own home.

Activities/Games:

(1) *Background Music:* Play the soundtrack from the musical as background music. If seeing a play, try to choose music from the historical period the play is set in.

(2) *Trivia:* Using colorful markers, decorate paper tablecloths with trivia questions pertaining to the musical. Some suggested questions: Who played the leading male role on Broadway? How long was the musical's run on Broadway? When did it run? Who wrote the music and lyrics? Who was the female lead in the screen version? Do you know all the words to the first verse of the theme song? As everyone eats, they can ask one another these questions and add their own.

(3) *Get There Early:* Read up on the play if you are unfamiliar with it. When you get to the theater, encourage everyone to read their programs. Then, discuss what the play or musical is about (without giving away its ending) to avoid any confusion about the plot.

More Ideas:

Oklahoma - Decorate using hay bales, wagon wheels, cowboy hats, quilts, and bandannas. Buffet menu suggestions: BBQ, baked beans, slaw, cake or brownies.

My Fair Lady - Seated dinner of roast beef, potatoes, salad, hard rolls and trifle. The table could be formal with china, linens, candlesticks and flowers. Top hats, canes, frilly ladies' hats, ruffled parasols and feather boas could also be used for decorations.

Oliver - Serve Fish 'n Chips on newspaper-covered tables lit by wooden candlesticks. Pour root beer into tin cups or frosted mugs.

The Music Man - Use patriotic colors, American flags, musical instruments as decorations with band leader's hat centerpiece. "Dinner on the Grounds" might include fried chicken, potato salad, rolls, and ice cream and cake.

The Great Outdoors

Guest List: Ages 11 to 13 (four to six depending on tent size).

Invitations: See page 116.

Favors: Small compass, whistle, flashlight or light stick given to kids to be used during the camp out.

Food: *Supper:* Hot dogs and buns, condiments, chips, snack food, peanut butter and crackers, fruit, plenty of canned drinks and S'mores for dessert. *S'mores:* Make sandwich using 2 graham crackers, and half of chocolate bar for each camper. Fill with hot, toasted marshmallow.
Breakfast: Biscuits on a stick or pastries from home, milk, orange juice, bacon, eggs, coffee, salt and pepper. Don't forget paper products.

Decorations: One wonderful part about an outdoor party is that nature has already done a magnificent job of decorating. Enjoy!

Tips:

1. Plan menus carefully and write them down.
2. Make a list of foods and equipment needed for the number of people to be served.
3. Pack food carefully so that it won't spoil or spill.
4. Store food properly before and after cooking.
5. Keep it simple.
6. Be safety conscious when working around a fire; have a container of water ready to put out fire when finished.
7. Have plenty of drinking water on hand.
8. Carry a first aid kit and bug spray.

Activities/Games:

(1) *Send-Off:* Have the guests meet at your home on afternoon of camp out. Have one vehicle packed with camping equipment and food. Use another vehicle to transport guests and their gear. Arrange for other parents to go along.

(2) *Camping Activities:* Drive to camp site, set up, take hikes, tell stories, sing around campfire, star gaze, wade in creek.

Setting up camp:

(1) Pitch tents on smooth, level ground.

(2) Take along tarpaulin to cover dining area and supplies.

(3) Gather firewood while daylight; stack under a shelter (bring along charcoal or stove just in case).

(4) Make sure everything is secure from animals before turning in for the night.

Biscuits-on-a-Stick:

You will need a roll of refrigerator biscuits, liquid butter or margarine, jelly and clean thick sticks. Roll dough of 1 biscuit into a "snake." Each camper twists the raw biscuit snake around the end of the stick. Bake over fire, turning often. When cooked, slide from stick, and pour butter and jelly into cavity left by stick. Delicious, messy, and fun!

① ② ③ ④

Mystery Party

A Neighborhood Scavenger Hunt

Guest List: Ages 11 and up.

Invitations: Poem and map of the neighborhood where the scavenger hunt will be held. "X" marks the address of the host. (See page 117.)

Favors: Silly prizes for the winning team are fun, such as animal noses or silly string.

Food: Popcorn, candy, chips and dip, pizza, cake, apple and cheese slices, soft drinks iced down in coolers.

Decorations: Use colorful paper products for table.

Rain Plan
Have plenty of large garbage bags on hand. Cut head and arm holes for guests to wear as rain gear.

Activities/Games:

Preparations: Make scavenger hunt list adapting Pirate Party (page 67) items for your neighborhood or even your yard. Consider writing cryptic word clues (perhaps in the form of a poem or riddle) to lead team players to each new clue until the mystery is solved. This is much more challenging, and involves kids really working together. Have available for each team a scavenger hunt list or cryptic clues, a map, and a shopping bag. A phone call to neighbors informing them of the hunt is courteous and helpful.

(1) *Ice-Breaker:* Have background music playing as guests arrive. Some guests may wish to bring tapes or CDs; be sure you approve of teen's music selection. Have a deck of cards, ping pong, or fooseball available, plus snack food to entertain guests until all arrive.

(2) *Neighborhood Scavenger Hunt:* Number teens off into teams of five or six for scavenger hunt. Assign an adult to each team and furnish them with a map on which the designated streets have been highlighted. Set a time limit. Allow enough time for hunt to be completed before dark. Give each team its list or clues, a map, and shopping bag. Explain the rules: no more than two items per house, one point per item unless otherwise marked. The winning team is the team back on time with the most items.

(3) *Refreshments:* As you tally points, teens help themselves to food and soft drinks.

Bonus Hunt:

After all teams have returned, ask teens to wait in driveway and give instructions for the bonus hunt. Teens go to houses on street of host to find an outrageous item that has been placed there before the party. When they find the owner of the item, they must ask for it in a specific manner in order to be given the item. Inform designated neighbor of correct key words necessary for the item. Example: "Hello, I am a friend of _____ and I am in need of a whatever." The outrageous item counts five points.

Healthy Party Snacks

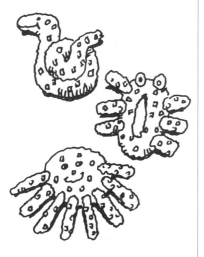

To some, parties mean candy, soda, cake, and ice cream. But many children today enjoy more healthful, less sugary alternatives and will gobble up grapes and raisins as fast as candy. Always provide healthful options in the foods and beverages you offer at a party.

Good-to-Eat Snacks:

pita bread sandwiches

cheese cubes

rolled ham slices

celery sticks (stuffed with cream
     cheese or peanut butter)

veggies and dip (cherry tomatoes,
     broccoli, celery, cauliflower,
     carrot sticks)

raisins

nuts (not for toddlers)

crackers

yogurt shakes

salsa and corn chips

pretzels

popcorn

rice cakes (spread with peanut
     butter)

bite-size muffins (blueberry, apple,
     banana)

fruits and dip (strawberries, grapes,
     apples slices, melon balls)

kabobs (fruit, cheese, vegetables,
     cooked meat)

- **Frozen Banana Treat:** Peel three bananas, cut in half crosswise, and insert a wooden stick into cut end. Freeze (about 30 minutes) on waxed paper. Melt 3/4 cup of chocolate chips and 1 1/2 tablespoons vegetable oil in a double boiler. One at a time, dip frozen bananas into chocolate mixture and roll in chopped nuts. Wrap in waxed paper and return to freezer. Makes 6 servings.
- **Spider Salad**: Put a canned peach half on a lettuce-lined plate. Decorate the spider using raisins for eyes, cherry stems for antennae, half a maraschino cherry slice for the mouth and carrot curls for legs. (Carrot Curls: Cut wide strips of carrot with a vegetable peeler, roll up each strip, fasten with toothpick, crisp in a bowl of ice water for a few minutes, drain, and remove the toothpick.)
- **Peanut Butter Bumblebee**: Mix one 18-ounce jar of smooth peanut butter with 6 tablespoons of honey and 3 cups of non-fat dry milk to form a soft dough. Shape 1 teaspoon of dough into an oval ball; press sliced almonds into sides for wings. Roll the shaft of a dampened tooth-pick in ground cinnamon. Make two small indentions for eyes, and press three lines across ball for bee's stripes, dipping toothpick into cinnamon each time.
- **Pretzel Animals**: In a large bowl, mix 1 package yeast, 1 1/2 cups warm water, 1 tablespoon sugar, and 1 table-spoon salt. Stir in 4 cups flour and knead on table until dough is smooth. Form dough into animal shapes. Brush with beaten egg and sprinkle with coarse salt. Bake in 425° oven for 15 minutes or until brown.

PARTIES *for* SPECIAL OCCASIONS

Earth Day Party

Topsoil Dessert

1 (8 oz.) pkg. cream
  cheese (softened)
1/2 stick butter (softened)
1/4 cup confectioners'
  sugar
1 (12 oz.) container
  whipped topping
2 (3 3/4 oz.) pkgs.
  vanilla pudding
2 1/4 cups milk
1 pound chocolate cream-
  filled cookies

Combine butter and
cream cheese; stir in
confectioners' sugar.
Fold in whipped topping.
Set aside. Mix vanilla
pudding and milk. Beat
until slightly stiff. Fold
into cream cheese
mixture. Crush cookies.
Set aside 1/3 of crumbs
for top. Stir remaining
crumbs into mixture.
Thoroughly wash clay
pots. Cover drainage
hole in bottom of pot with
foil or waxed paper. Pour
mixture into individual
pots or one large
container. Sprinkle
crumbs on top.

Earth Day is a symbol of envi-
ronmental responsibility and
stewardship. It is observed
internationally on April 22.

Guest List: Ages 7 to 12.

Invitations: See page 117.

Favors: Natural items made
at party plus items having
earth or globe motif such as
pencils, pencil sharpeners, yo-
yos, stickers, erasers and
puzzles.

Food: Lemonade and topsoil
dessert made in individual clay
pots or one large container.

Decorations: Cover picnic
tables in brown paper. Use a
glove and fresh garden flowers
for centerpiece. Use earth-
colored, all-natural fiber paper
products.

Activities/Games:

(1) *Nature on Clay:* Adult provides items from nature (leaves, flowers, grasses), any type clay (drying and non-drying kinds both work), and rolling pins. Roll clay smooth and 1/2-inch thick. Carefully press natural items on clay. Gently remove items from clay. The items will leave beautiful patterns and imprints. Using a toothpick put child's initials on the bottom.

(2) *Mini-Greenhouse:* Things you need:
- 2 clear plastic cups (same size) that hold at least nine ounces
- potting soil
- water
- rubber cement
- clear tape
- straight pin or nail
- a half-dozen seeds (radish, squash, tomato, sunflower seeds work well)

Half-fill one plastic cup with dirt. Plant seeds in dirt. Water soil with a few tablespoons of water. Punch holes in top of other cup with nail or pin. Cover holes with transparent tape. Coat rims of both cups with cement. Wait a few minutes and then put cups together. Add an extra coat of cement to the outside rim of cups for a perfect seal. Place in the sun. Check often; water through holes when needed. When plant outgrows greenhouse, remove top.

(3) *Sponge Sprouters:* Things you need:
- string
- push pins or thumbtacks
- water mister (spray bottle)
- scissors
- a natural sponge (obtain at a beauty, automotive, or art supply store)
- seeds: parsley, mustard, bean, alfalfa

Cut a section of sponge about 3 inches. Soak the sponge in water. Squeeze out extra water so sponge doesn't drip. Push seeds into the holes of sponge. Tie the string around the sponge and knot it securely. Instruct kids to hang sponge (using a tack) in front of a window at home, so the sponge gets lots of light. Keep sponge moist by misting it everyday. Watch it sprout!

(4) *Green Up:* Give groups of children a garbage bag. Send groups up and down neighborhood with an adult and pick up all litter along way. Talk about taking care of the Earth and keeping it clean. Make up a rap about "The Good Earth." Wash hands when kids return to the party.

Help a Bird Make a Nest

Help a bird gather materials for its nest. Tie several pine cones in a tree with string. Hang pieces of yarn and thin strips of fabric in the pine cones.

Natural Dyes

Make tie-dye socks or t-shirts using natural dyes.

Yellow = goldenrod, pomegranate rind, onion skins, willow leaves, marigolds

Red = cherries, birch bark (gathered from the ground only)

Purple = blackberries, elderberries

Green = carrot tops, spinach, moss, grass clippings

Tear plant materials into small pieces and cover with water. Ask a grown-up to boil 5—20 minutes to reach desired color intensity. Add 1 tablespoon vinegar to set dye. Cool before dyeing clothes.

Christmas Caroling Party

Candy Cane Reindeer: Moveable eyes, small pom-poms for noses, and chenille pipe cleaners are available at craft stores.

Guest List: All ages. This is a great party to include entire families or other large groups such as school classes or church youth groups in the elementary or junior high age group.

Invitations: See page 118.

Favors: Have a large jar filled with candy canes or candy cane reindeer by the door to hand out as guests leave.

Food: Top off the evening's festivities with plenty of hot chocolate or cider, as well as snack foods and pick-up desserts.

Decorations: Your home will be decorated for Christmas, so additional decorations are unnecessary.

Activities/Game:

Preparations: Before the party, contact those to whom you will be caroling, such as teachers, elderly neighbors or nursing home residents. Line up drivers ahead of time. Thread large-eyed needles with dental floss or button thread in three- to four-foot lengths for popcorn stringing. Have plenty of song sheets available for caroling.

(1) *Popcorn Stringing:* While waiting for everyone to arrive, string popcorn for the Christmas tree. Supply guests with a threaded darning needle. Be sure to have plenty of popcorn, not all of it will make it on the strings!

(2) *Caroling:* Hand out song sheets; rehearse songs. Drive to destination. Sing the first verse of two or three songs and end with "WE WISH YOU A MERRY CHRISTMAS." A few strong adult voices are helpful. Don't sing too long; it's awkward for person being sung to.

Nancy's Easy Turtles:
Line a baking sheet with wax paper. Space pecan halves about two inches apart. Thinly slice candy-making caramel and press over each pecan half. Butter hands to make the job easier. Melt candy-making chocolate in the microwave by placing chocolate wafers in a microwave bowl and microwaving for 2 minutes at half power; then stir. Continue microwaving for 30 second intervals, stirring after each interval, until wafers are smooth and melted. Spoon chocolate over pecans and caramel. When set, remove and store at room temperature. Candy-making caramel and chocolate are available at cake decorating stores.

Favorite Cookie Swap

Cookies are a favorite with kids and a good excuse for a party.

Kids bring three dozen cookies and the recipe to share with others at the party. Everyone tastes the cookies and copies down the recipes they want. Host adult should provide index cards and pens.

Guest List: Ages 8 and up. Limit the number, consider space limitations for activities and cookie swap when inviting guests.

Invitations: See page 119.

Favors: Swapped cookies to take home.

Food: Hot chocolate, punch, nuts, mints, popcorn.

Decorations: Streamers and balloons.

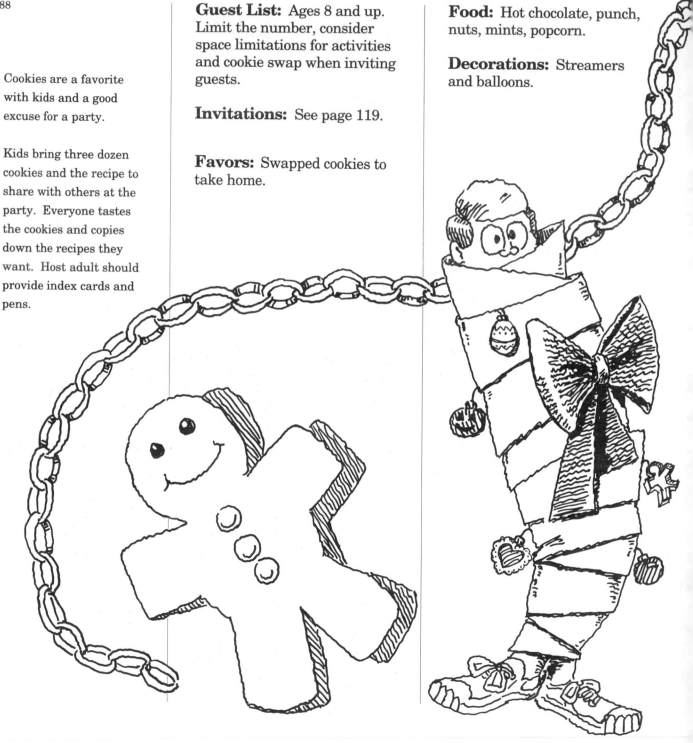

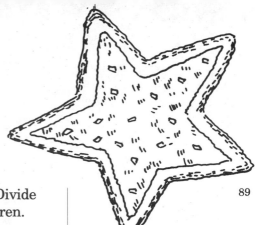

Activities/Games:

(1) *Cookie Swap:* Display cookies on table as guests arrive. Just before time to go home, give each guest a box and let them go around the table and choose two of each kind of cookie until they have all been taken. (Host should make about six batches of different kinds of cookies to add to selection.) Everyone should go home with at least as many cookies as they brought, if not more.

(2) *Crepe Paper Wrap:* Divide into teams of 5 or 6 children. The tallest member of the team is to be wrapped; others are the decorators. Have children take colorful crepe paper and wrap until all rolls have been completely used. Decorate wrapped person with a few nonbreakable decorations. First group to use all materials is winner. Take lots of pictures! (Large rolls of crepe paper may be excessive. Unwind, divide, and rewind into smaller, more manageable rolls prior to the party.)

(3) *Sweat Suit Balloon Stuff:* Divide children into groups of six. Have shortest child in each group put on an extra large sweat suit over clothing. On signal the remaining children in the group stuff 20 to 30 balloons (pre-blown and stored in garbage bags) into each sweat suit. Call time after one minute. To declare winner, adult takes a needle and <u>carefully</u> sticks it through sweat suit to pop balloons. Have children count the "pops." The most "pops" wins.

Cookie Stack

Use flat-surfaced sandwich cookies. Children take turns stacking the cookies one at a time to build a tower. See which team can use the most cookies to build the highest tower.

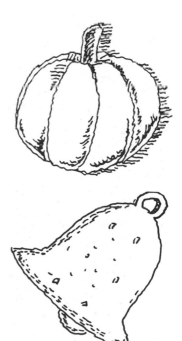

Valentine Party

Guest List: All ages.

Invitations: See page 120.

Favors: Red wax lips, red lollipops, waffle cones filled with candy and wrapped in plastic wrap or red cellophane, tied with red or pink yarn.

Food: Gutter Ice Cream Sundaes (see page 91) and soft drinks.

Decorations: Use red, pink and white crepe paper streamers, balloons and homemade hearts to carry out the theme.

Sweet Hearts:

A fun homemade valentine greeting or favor is a personalized heart cookie. Purchase a large heart-shaped cookie cutter. Prepare rolled cookie recipe and cut dough into heart shapes. Bake and cool. Decorate with a message or individual's name. Children love to make and receive these valentines!

Bright, Shiny Icing:

If you want vivid colors instead of pastels for your icing, try this *before* you bake the cookies:

In a small individual custard cup, drop an egg yolk and a few drops of food coloring; stir. Add a little water (2 teaspoons) to make the icing more "paintable." Do the same for each color.

Using a small paint-brush for each color, paint one color at a time; let dry before applying next color.

Bake the cookie according to package directions. Colors come out bright and shiny.

Activities/Games:

(1) *Mended Hearts:* As each guest arrives give him or her half of a commercial valentine. After all arrive they are to find the person who has the matching half. These two children will be partners while making sundaes.

(2) *Spoon and String Relay Games:* Divide children into two groups. Securely tie a skein of red yarn to end of spoon. Give spoon and skein of yarn to each team. First person in line puts spoon inside front of shirt and down pants leg then passes spoon to next person in line. Keep feeding string from first person in line to next until spoon has passed through each person's clothing to the last child in line. First team to finish wins.

(3) *Sundae in the Gutter:* Before the party, buy plastic gutters and have them cut into six or eight foot lengths from local building supply. Wash and dry. Use vinyl tablecloth for easy cleanup. Have children line up on either side of table, partners facing each other. Furnish ice cream, nuts, cherries, chocolate sauce, whipped cream, etc. Have all contribute to making sundae in the gutter. After children complete their sundaes, take one quick picture and signal READY-GO-EAT!

(4) *Almost a Kiss:* Divide into teams. Each child holds a straw in his or her mouth. On signal, pass a circle candy from one straw to the next down the line until the last player has it.

Easter Egg Treasure Hunt

Make party one hour for ages 4 to 7; 1 1/2 hours for ages 8 to 10.

Guest List: Ages 4 to 10.

Invitations: Cut construction paper egg, folded on one edge. Child can help decorate invitations with colored markers. Put party information on inside. If guests are to bring their own Easter baskets, be sure to tell them (put their name on the bottom). (See page 120.)

Favors: Eggs and treasure found on hunt.

Food: Bunny cake and punch.

Decorations: Identify the party house with plastic eggs hung from branches of a small tree in front yard.

Activities/Games:

(1) *Bunny Puppets:* As young children arrive, they make bunny puppets. Pre-cut face and ears from construction paper. Glue moveable eyes and pom-pom noses to face. Glue completed bunny face to tongue depressor. Moveable eyes, pom-poms and tongue depressors are available at craft stores.

(2) *Egg Bags:* Instead of bringing their own baskets, have older children make sacks out of gallon-size zippered storage bags. Supply Easter grass and large egg-shaped plain stickers and markers for names.

(3) *Easter Egg Treasure Hunt:* Fill plastic eggs with candy or coupons to use at the store that you have created. Show children the store that consists of tables arranged with prizes.

Explain boundaries and rules: If the child finds an egg with a prize coupon in it, it can be kept until the end or immediately cash it in at the store for a prize.

Bunny Cake

1. Prepare and bake cake mix in two 8- or 9-inch round cake pans as directed on package. Cool.
2. Cut cake as shown. Ice sides of each cake piece.
3. Assemble pieces as shown on a cookie sheet or tray or 18" x 15" foil-covered cardboard. Ice cake top.
4. Sprinkle about 2 2/3 cups coconut onto sides.
5. Dye coconut pink and green. In plastic bag, mix 3/4 cup coconut with a few drops of red food coloring. Work with hands until color is evenly distributed. Repeat with 1 1/4 cups coconut and a few drops of green food coloring.
6. Sprinkle pink coconut over ears and bow tie; sprinkle green coconut evenly around cake.
7. Use jelly beans for eyes and nose. Use licorice sticks for whiskers.

Watermelon Party

Pool or backyard summer party

Guest List: All ages.

Invitations: Watermelon shape cut by children out of construction paper. (See page 121.)

Favors: Sunglasses, visors, water toys, balloons.

Food: Watermelon!! Watermelon cookie or red velvet cake with green and pink icing. Punch or lemonade. And a Bucket of Lunch.

Decorations: Set your table with red and white checked tablecloth, red plates and napkins. Watermelon baskets, balloons, and summer flowers could be used to enhance the festive mood.

A Bucket of Lunch:
Here's a great idea, if the party occurs around lunch time! Purchase beach pails in a variety of colors. Put ice and pre-cooled soft drinks into a plastic zip bag in the bottom of each bucket. Place wrapped sandwiches and chip bags on top.

JUST for FUN

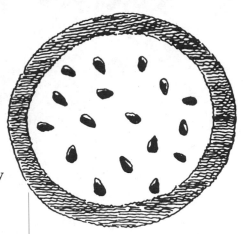

Activities/Games:

(1) *Seed Guess:* Guess the number of watermelon seeds in a jar.

2) *Seed Spit:* Watermelon seed spitting contest. As guests eat watermelon they save their seeds in small cups provided. Let the contest begin! Kids see who can spit a seed the furthest.

(3) *Watermelon Relay:* If party is at a pool, have a relay pushing floating melons around in the pool. Yes, watermelons do float!

(4) *Water Play:* For young children provide a lawn water slide with supervision or wading pools and plenty of water toys.

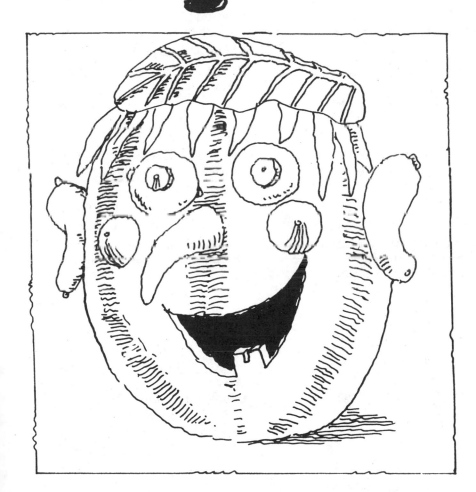

Lynn's Watermelon Cookie:

Press one 34-ounce roll of chocolate chip cookie dough into pizza pan. (To do this, cut dough into 3/8" slices and place them in the pan. Cover the slices with a piece of wax paper and press the slices together into one big cookie. Remove wax paper.) Bake at 350° until done. Decorate the center with pink icing and green icing around the edge as shown. Use chocolate chips for seeds.

Watermelon Person Centerpiece:

Use your imagination with fresh fruits and vegetables to create your own character.
Suggestions:
Red or yellow pepper nose
Lemon half with olive eyes
Radish cheeks
Squash ears
Carrot strip hair
Red cabbage leaf hat.

TRADITIONS

Traditions have a way of just evolving over time. Often they begin when your family does something spontaneously. Later someone says "let's do it again," and before you know it a tradition is born!

Webster's Dictionary defines "tradition" as a handing down of information, beliefs and customs by word of mouth or by example from one generation to another.

Ours is a world where traditions are easily trampled. Since most parents want their children to have some of the experiences they had as children, we encourage you to try some of your old family traditions—even those you only vaguely remember now—in starting your own.

Listed below are some traditions to get you started.

(1) *Family Reunion Talent Show or Play.* Anytime extended family comes together the children organize and put on a play or show. This entertains the children while the adults visit, and provides an opportunity for the children to get to know each other better.

(2) *Birthday Meal for Family.* The birthday child picks out favorite foods for the menu. Anything goes—after all, it's the birthday person's choice!

(3) *Birthday Gifts at Breakfast.* Before breakfast, stack the birthday person's chair at the table with all the birthday cards and gifts.

(4) *Money Cake.* Child's favorite birthday cake with cellophane-wrapped new coins on top. Guess who gets to keep the coins ?!

(5) *Banners.* This is a way of making an event special. Make banners for birthdays, homecomings, special achievements, welcomings or spend-the-night guests!

(6) *Streamers.* Here is a decorating tradition that can be started and kept from year to year. Attach colorful, crepe paper streamers at two or three foot intervals around the edge of the ceiling. Drape twisted streamers and gather them in the center of room and attach to ceiling or chandelier. Add balloons.

(7) *Tie a Yellow Ribbon Around a Tree.* Appropriate for welcoming someone home. We have used ribbon, crepe paper and found that an old yellow lawn water slide works great!

(8) *"You Are Special" Plate.* This is a special plate recognizing the honoree's accomplishment or special event. You can purchase a special plate or just designate a certain plate you already own as the "special plate."

(9) *Decorate Birthday Child's Room.* On the eve of the birthday (after the child is asleep), the parents and siblings decorate the room with balloons and crepe paper.

(10) *From Toe to Present.* After the birthday child is asleep, tie a string around his or her big toe. Wind the string throughout the house, over furniture and around corners to a special present. This is usually the "biggie," the present the child has been wanting!

(11) *Indoor Easter Morning Treasure Hunt.* This is an Easter egg hunt using separate clues hidden in plastic eggs for each child. Each clue sends the child to a specific place in the house where he or she will find another clue and a present or two along the way.

(12) *May Day Baskets.* Weave colorful paper baskets of construction paper and fill with wild violets or other flowers. Leave on neighbors' doors.

(13) *Halloween Treats.* What began as a safe alternative to "trick or treating" in the street has turned into an annual neighborhood event. The children bob for apples, decorate masks, and enjoy popcorn balls. "Traditionally," the popcorn balls are made with colorful gum drop halves instead of the usual caramel.

(14) *Tea for Two.* Plan to have tea and cookies with a senior neighbor the first Sunday of each month. Talk about the old days and exchange stories.

(15) *Annual Bike Ride.* On the first day of summer, gather together with family and friends for a bicycle ride in the country. Equip bikes with old bells and horns for fun.

Take a winter morning snowshoe walk or x-country ski with family. Fill a thermos with cocoa and put in a backpack for a warm treat on the trek.

Halloween Popcorn Balls

1 cup butter or margarine
1 pound marshmallows
5 quarts of popped corn
1 bag bite-sized orange
    gumdrops

Melt butter and marshmallows over low heat. Stir until melted. Add popped corn and gum drops. Butter hands well. Form popcorn balls. Let dry. Wrap in wax paper and twist ends to close. Rewrap in colorful cellophane.

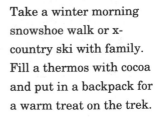

Hint for Luminaries:
The bottom of a two-liter, clear plastic drink bottle is a good stabilizer inside the bag or can be used alone. Add sand and a votive candle.
A long-handled butane fireplace lighter works well for lighting the candles inside the bags.

(16) *Getting the Christmas Tree.* Whether you cut your own or purchase one, make it a tradition. Go the same weekend each year and end your outing with hot chocolate and Christmas cookies.

(17) *Exploring.* Explore historical sights in your state with your family. Each summer, take a couple of day trips to visit different places of significance. Pack a picnic lunch.

(18) *Glitter and Glue.* Make homemade cards for Mother's Day, Father's Day, and family birthdays. Have art supplies on hand—construction paper, glitter, glue, markers, old magazines or family photos— for kids to use for crafting the cards. The time spent on homemade cards make them extra meaningful.

(19) *Where to?* Take an annual day hike. Let the kids decide where to venture. Pack food, bathing suits, towels, and bug spray for the trip. And don't forget the camera!

(20) *New Year's Eve Tradition.* Leave your boot or shoe for Father Time to fill with candy.

(21) *Weekend Breakfasts.* Let a family member be the cook for special breakfasts of doughnuts, pancakes in fun shapes, or French toast.

(22) *Traditional Recipes.* Red velvet cake for Fourth of July; cut-out cookies for Valentine's Day, caramel apples and popcorn balls at Halloween.

Invitation Sampler

These are simple ideas for you to copy; feel free to customize the concepts for your child's party.

To make it easy, these designs are set up for 4 1/4" x 5 1/2" cards; four cards will fit on an 8 1/2" x 11" piece of paper. Art and information are on one side, so that you can address the card on the other side.

Make sure the copy paper you use meets postal standards. If you aren't sure it will go through the mail as a postcard, take a piece of the paper you want to use to the post office and ask a clerk, or plan to send the invitations in envelopes.

All of these drawings are made to fit a 4 3/8" x 5 3/4" envelope. A printer or stationery store would know it as an A-2 envelope. If you want your invitation to be larger, most printers and office supply stores have copiers or equipment that can enlarge the artwork to a variety of sizes.

Most of these invitations can be redesigned to a folded invitation format with art on the front and information on the inside.

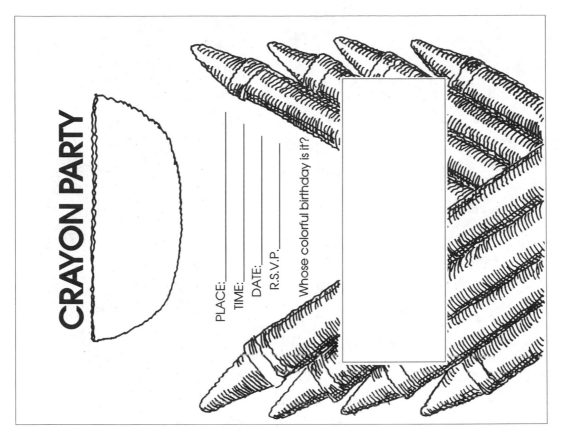

CRAYON PARTY

Whose colorful birthday is it?

R.S.V.P._____

DATE:_____

TIME:_____

PLACE:_____

Crayon Party

Write the guest's name in the space at the top of the card. Make a dot-to-dot drawing of the birthday child's name in the space at the bottom.

STOP

FOR _____'s

BIRTHDAY !!!!!

The light's on go

For a Birthday of fun.

Please come on over,

We'll stay on the run.

Bring your favorite riding toy,

And please don't be late.

We'll Stop, Look & Listen

On the following date.

DATE:_____

TIME:_____

PLACE:_____

Stop, Look & Listen Party

102

Dinosaur Party

See page 16 for more ideas.

Surprise, Surprise!
Come in with a roar!

It's _____'s
Dinosaur Birthday!
And now we'll tell you more.

_____

Time: _____

Date: _____

Place: _____

Trash Bash

See page 18 for more ideas.

It's a **TRASH BASH**
so come on along.
You'll learn what we're
doing to our earth
that is wrong!
We'll recycle trash and
have fun while we do it!
You'll go home with ideas
of how to reuse it.

Date _____

Time _____

Place _____

_____

Occasion _____

_____

_____

HAPPY BIRTHDAY
from
Friends around the World

Hoy Es To Dia

Buon Compleanno

Friends from near, Friends from far, Friends are Friends wherever they are.

Come celebrate _____'s Birthday
dressed in a costume from another country.
Bring a snack from that country, too!

Date _____ Time_____

Place_____

Szcze,´sliwych urodzin

Friends around the World

See page 20 for more ideas.

HAPPY BIRTHDAY!

JOIN THE PARADE!

for

_____'s Birthday

Date _____ Time_____

Place_____

_____

Everyone Loves a Parade

Go Fish

See page 24 for other ideas.

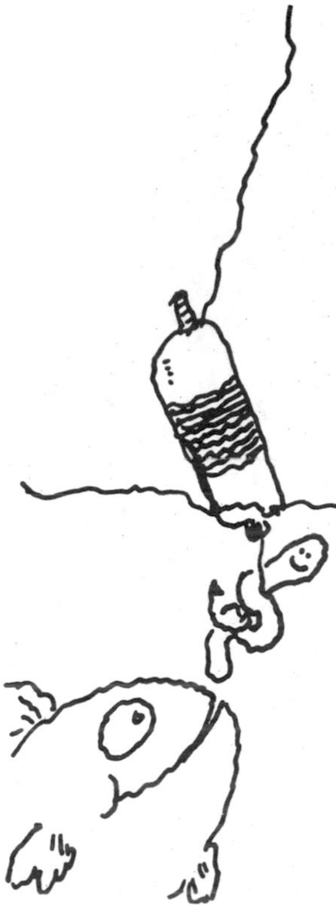

It's my birthday, so let's

GO FISH

in _____'s backyard pond

at _____

from _____ o'clock until _____ o'clock

on _____ the _____ of _____.

We'll be reeling in some big surprises!

Call _____ if you cannot come.

You belong in a zoo!

Join _____
for a birthday party!
on _____
the _____ of _____
from _____ 'til _____ o'clock.
Meet at _____
_____.

Rain date:_____
time:_____

Zoo Party

Glue half of a peanut shell to the end of the elephant's trunk and a tuft of yarn for the tail.

BIRTHDAY PARTY!

For _____
_____
Time _____ 'til _____
Date _____
_____
Place _____
_____
Wear your swimsuit.
Bring a towel.
Call _____,
if you can't come.

Fun-in-the-Sun Party

See page 28 for other ideas.

**Old West
Party**

To personalize
your card, take
a photo of your
child in western
wear and cover
the cartoon in
the middle.
Reproduce on
copy machine.

All Dudes & Gals

WANTED

for_____ Birthday!

_____   _____
(date)   (time)

Saddle Up & Head West to

_____
(location)

Wear jeans or a western get-up.
We'll provide a cowboy hat for each buckaroo!

If you're going to be hung up and
can't come, call _____.

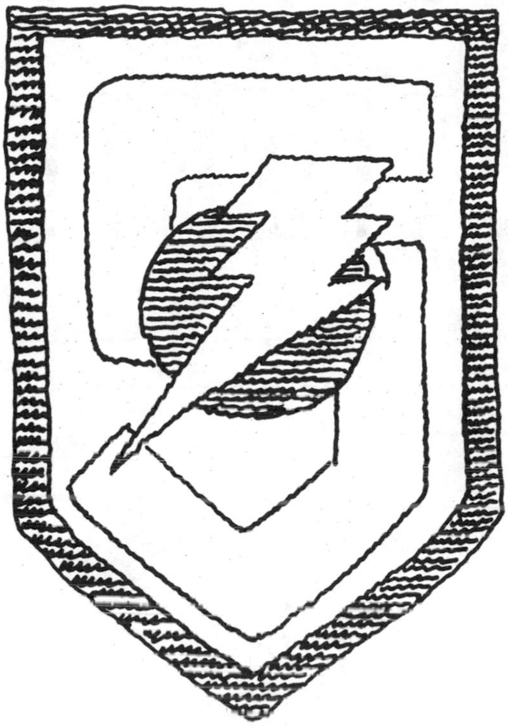

SUPER HERO PARTY

When?_____
_____
Where?_____
_____
Why?_____
_____
Why not? Regrets, call:_____

Snow or Sand Sculpture Party

See page 38 for more ideas.

COME BUILD A CASTLE!

Date_____ Time_____

Place_____

Bring_____

Backyard Camping Party

Happy Birthday

_____

Come camp-out in my backyard!

Date & Time: from_____

'til _____

Location   Bring

_____   _____

_____   _____

_____

Time Capsule Party

Make it a date:_____

Don't be late:_____

Location:_____

Bring:_____

Event:_____

R.S.V.P._____

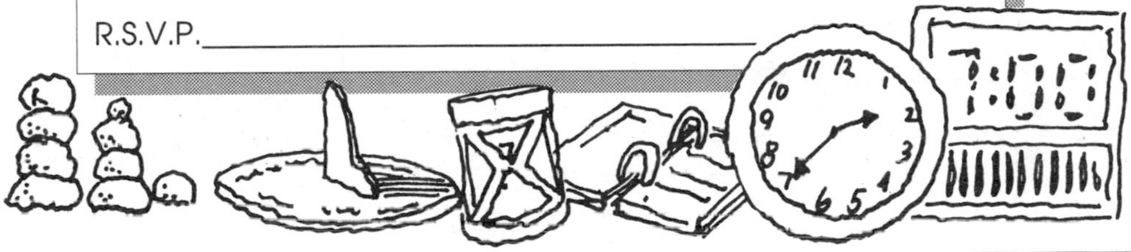

**Time Capsule
Party**

Come reel 'em in!

It's _____'s Birthday!

We're goin' fishin' _____ at _____.
　　　　　　　　　　DATE　　　　　　　　TIME

Meet us at _____.

Bring_____.

R.S.V.P._____

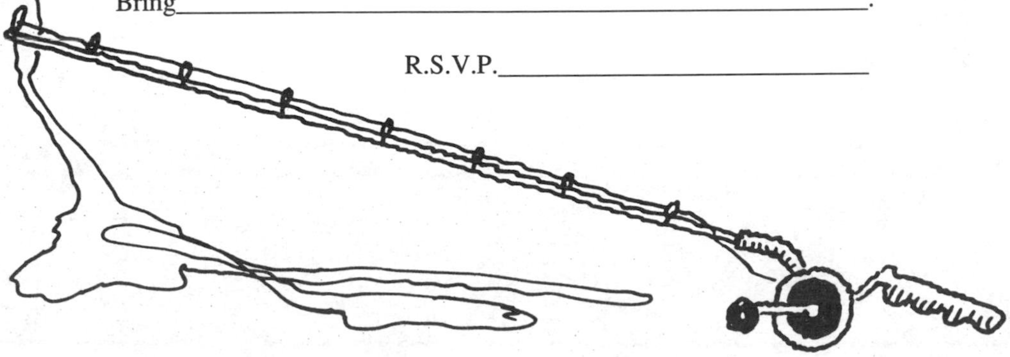

**Gone Fishin'
Party**

**Bake Your
Own Cake**

Bake Your Own Birthday Cake Party

In the KITCHEN of :

Date:

Time:

Location:

(Please come; you can lick the spoon!)

R.S.V.P. :

Movie Night

Be sure to tell the parents the name of the movie. Fill in the title at the bottom of the card.

MOVIE NIGHT

Occasion: _____

Date: _____

Time: _____

Location:_____

Bring: _____

RSVP: _____

HAPPY BIRTHDAY

(Hold up to a mirror to read.)

_____ WHO?

_____ WHERE?

_____

_____ WHEN?

_____

Come dressed backwards!

Backwards Party

See page 52 for more information.

GAME DATE:_____

TIME:_____

FIELD:_____

_____

COME TO

_____

BASEBALL•BIRTHDAY PARTY!

BRING:_____

_____

If you can't join us in the dugout, call

_____

(Rain Date:_____)

Baseball Game Party

112

Sock Hop Party

Change second and third lines to rhyme with the child's age. Example:

So be on time!

_____ is turning 9.

So don't be late!

_____ is turning 8.

It's a Birthday Sock Hop,

_____

_____

_____

We'll Boogie, we'll Woogie,
And do the Twist.
If you don't come,
You'll surely be missed!

_____ *is the date,*
_____ *'til* _____ *is the time.*
Please come to my house,
That's the end of my rhyme!

Soccer Party

We're celebrating

_____'s

BIRTHDAY!

So, come join us for breakfast; then we'll all go to the baseball card show.

On _____, we'll pick you up at

_____

and bring you home at

_____.

(Adult supervision will be provided.)

R.S.V.P. _____

Bring baseball cards to trade or sell and spending money.

Breakfast and Baseball Card Show / Party

If you have a photo of your child in a baseball uniform, cover the cartoon on this card with your photo and reproduce on a copy machine.

AHOY MATES!!!

IT'S _____'S

BIRTHDAY!

WE'RE FLYING THE JOLLY ROGER & SETTING SAIL TO SCAVENGE THE SEAS.

MEET AT THIS TIME: _____

ON THIS DAY: _____

AT THIS SPOT: _____

_____

IF YOU CAN'T BE A MEMBER OF OUR CREW, CALL THE CROW'S NEST AT:

_____

Pirate Scavenger Hunt / Party

Sleep-Over Party

Fill in moon, stars, and title with colored markers or metallic paints.

SLEEP-OVER PARTY

Occasion_____

Date_____Time_____

Location_____

Bring_____

R.S.V.P._____

Pen Pal Party

FROM:

_____

ADDRESS: _____

_____

TO:

_____

DATE of Party:_____

TIME:_____

R.S.V.P._____

ATTN: It's a PEN PAL PARTY!

You are cordially invited to a

GET ACQUAINTED • BACK-TO-SCHOOL
PARTY

Date_____ Time_____

Place_____

R.S.V.P._____

Hosts

_____ _____

_____ _____

_____ _____

Get Acquainted, Back-to-School Party

See page 72 for more ideas.

Spaghetti under the Stars

Celebrating

_____'s _____ birthday

Date:_____

Time: _____

Address: _____

_____

Spaghetti under the Stars Dinner Party

See page 74 for more ideas.

Pre-Theater Dinner / Party

See page 76 for more ideas.

Join us before the

FOOTLIGHTS

Date_____

Time_____

Place_____

for a Dinner and Theater Party
celebrating _____!

R.S.V.P. _____

The Great Outdoors Party

CAMP OUT!!!

We're getting away to celebrate...

_____!!!

FROM: Time_____ Date_____
UNTIL: Time_____ Date_____
MEET AT: _____
_____
BRING:_____
_____
_____

If you can't join us around our campfire,
please call _____.

MYSTERY PARTY

Marks the spot
For a few good friends - not a lot.

For a scavenger hunt, pizza, and fun!
It won't be a party without you, so please come!

Occasion _____

Date _____ Time _____

Location _____

R.S.V.P.: _____

Mystery Party

Draw a map of your neighborhood with an X marking the location of the party. The party information can be copied on the back.

Earth Day BIRTHDAY!

It's _____Birthday!

Date:_____

Time:_____

Location:_____

R.S.V.P._____

Earth Day Party

**Christmas
Caroling
Party**

C O O K I E   S W A P

Date _____

Time _____

Location _____

*Bring 3 dozen homemade cookies on a tray,
plus the recipe.*

R.S.V.P. _____

**Valentine
Party**

Be ᴬᵀ My Valentine Party

_____
PLACE

_____
TIME

_____
DATE

_____
R.S.V.P.

_____
HOST

**Easter Egg
Treasure Hunt**

Fill in with
crayons or colored
markers; draw
your own designs.
See page 92 for
more ideas.

EASTER EGG
TREASURE HUNT

_____
PLACE

_____
TIME

_____
DATE

_____
BRING

_____
IF YOU CAN'T HOP OVER, PLEASE CALL

_____
HOSTS

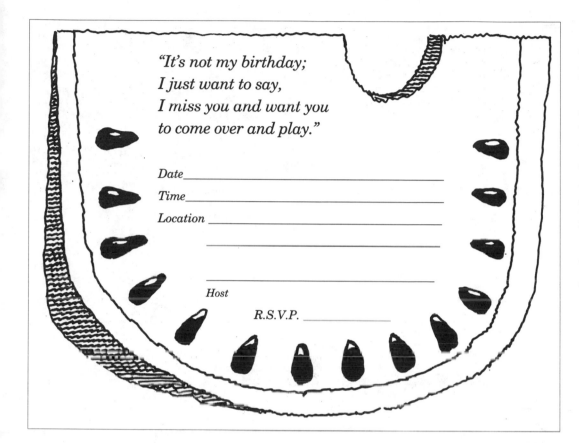

"It's not my birthday;
I just want to say,
I miss you and want you
to come over and play."

Date_____

Time_____

Location _____

_____

_____

Host

R.S.V.P. _____

Watermelon Party

Another idea for this invitation is to copy the art on the front of a card folded at the top with the information on the inside. Tear out the bite with your thumb.

Invitation Index

Recipe Index

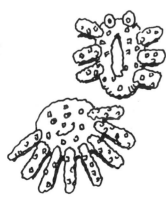

Activity/Game Index

More Good Books from Williamson Publishing

To order additional copies of **Great Parties for Kids,** please enclose $10.95 per copy plus $2.50 for shipping. Follow "To Order" instructions on the last page. Thank you.

ADVENTURES IN ART
Art & Craft Experiences for 7- to 14-Year-Olds
by Susan Milord

Imagine an art book that encourages children to explore, to experience, to touch and to see, to learn and to create...imagine a true adventure in art. Here's a book that teaches artisans' skills without stifling creativity. Covers making handmade papers, puppets, masks, paper seascapes, seed art, tin can lantern, berry ink, still life, silk screen, batiking, carving, and so much more. Perfect for the older child. Let the adventure begin!

160 pages, 11 x 8 1/2, 500 illustrations
Quality paperback, $12.95

ECOART!
Earth-Friendly Art & Craft Experiences for 3- to 9-Year-Olds
by Laurie Carlson

What better way to learn to love and care for the Earth than through creative art play! Laurie Carlson's latest book is packed with 150 projects using only recyclable, reusable, or nature's own found art materials. These fabulous activities are sure to please any child!

160 pages, 11 x 8 1/2, 400 illustrations
Quality paperback, $12.95

THE KIDS' MULTICULTURAL ART BOOK
Art & Craft Experiences from Around the World
by Alexandra M. Terzian

Winner of
The Parents' Choice Gold Award

Alexandra Terzian brings an unsurpassed enthusiasm to the hands-on multicultural art experience. Children will reach across continents and oceans with paper, paste, and paints, while absorbing basic sensibilities about the wondrous cultures of others. Children will learn by making such things as the *Korhogo Mud Cloth* and the *Wodaabe Mirror Pouch* from Africa, the *Chippewa Dream Catcher* of the American Indian, the *Kokeshi Doll* of Japan, *Chinese Egg Painting,* the Mexican *Folk Art Tree of Life,* the *Twirling Palm Puppet* from India, and the Guatemalan *Green Toad Bank.* A virtual feast of multicultural art and craft experiences!

160 pages, 11 x 8 1/2, over 400 how-to-do-it illustrations
Quality paperback, $12.95

Here's a cookbook written for kids by two teenagers who know what kids like to eat! *Kids Cook!* is filled with over 150 recipes for great tasting foods that kids ages 8 and up can cook for themselves and for their families and friends, too. Try breakfast bonanzas like *Breakfast Sundaes,* great lunches including *Chicken Shirt Pocket,* super salads like *A Whale of a Fruit Salad,* quick snacks and easy extras like *Nacho Nibbles,* delicious dinners including *Pizza Originale,* and dynamite desserts and soda fountain treats including *Chocolate Surprise Cupcakes.* All recipes are for "real," healthy foods - not cutesy recipes that are no fun to eat. Plus Nutri Notes, Safety First, and plenty of special menus for Father's Day, Grandma's Teatime, picnics, and parties. One terrific book!

176 pages, 11 x 8 1/2, over 150 recipes, illustrations
Quality paperback, $12.95

KIDS COOK!
Fabulous Food for
the Whole Family
by Sarah Williamson
and Zachary
Williamson

The latest book by award-winning author Susan Milord invites children to experience, taste, and embrace the daily lives of children from the far corners of the earth. In 365 days of experiences, it tears down stereotypes and replaces them with the fascinating realities of our differences and our similarities. Children everywhere can plant and grow, write and tell stories, draw and craft, cook and eat, sing and dance, look and explore, as they learn to live in an atmosphere of global respect and cultural awareness that is born of personal experience.

160 pages, 11 x 8 1/2, over 400 illustrations
Quality paperback, $12.95

HANDS AROUND
THE WORLD
365 Creative Ways
to Build Cultural
Awareness &
Global Respect
by Susan Milord

Winner of the Parents' Choice Gold Award for learning and doing books, *The Kids' Nature Book* is loved by children, grandparents, and friends alike. Simple projects and activities emphasize fun while quietly reinforcing the wonder of the world we all share. Packed with facts and fun!

160 pages, 11 x 8 1/2, 425 illustrations
Quality paperback, $12.95

Over 200,000
copies sold!
THE KIDS'
NATURE BOOK
365 Indoor/Out-
door Activities
and Experiences
by Susan Milord

Over 250,000 copies sold!

KIDS CREATE!
Art & Craft Experiences for 3- to 9-Year-Olds
by Laurie Carlson

What's the most important experience for children ages 3 to 9? Why, to create something by themselves. Carlson provides over 150 creative experiences ranging from making dinosaur sculptures to clay cactus gardens, from butterfly puppets to windsocks. Plenty of help for the parents working with the kids, too! A delightfully innovative book.

160 pages, 11 x 8 1/2, over 400 illustrations
Quality paperback, $12.95

KIDS AND WEEKENDS!
Creative Ways to Make Special Days
by Avery Hart and Paul Mantell

Packed with truly creative ways to play, have fun, learn, grow, and build self-esteem and positive relationships, this book is a must for every parent, grandparent, babysitter and teacher. Hart and Mantell will inspire us all to transform some part of every weekend - even if it is only 30 minutes - into a special experience. Everything from backyard nature to putting on a magic show to creating a bird sanctuary to writing a book about yourself to environmentally-sound activities indoors and out. Whatever your interests, no matter how busy you are, kids and their families will savor special weekend moments.

176 pages, 11 x 8 1/2, over 400 illustrations
Quality paperback, $12.95

KIDS MAKE MUSIC!
Clapping and Tapping from Bach to Rock
by Avery Hart and Paul Mantell

No instruments necessary - just hands, feet, and wiggly bodies! Kids are natural music makers, and with the kid-loving music makers, Avery Hart and Paul Mantell, children everywhere will be doing the *Dinosaur Dance,* singing the *Dishwashin' Blues,* cleaning their rooms to *Rap,* belting it out in a *Jug Band* or *An Accidental Orchestra,* putting on a *Fairy Tale Opera,* learning to *Tap Dance* or creating a *Bona Fide Ballet* (homemade tutu included)! Those hands will be clapping, those feet will be tapping, those faces will be grinning, and they may be humming anything from Bach to Rock.

160 pages, 11 x 8 1/2, with hundreds of illustrations
Quality paperback, $12.95

THE KIDS' WILDLIFE BOOK
Exploring Animal Worlds through Indoor/Outdoor Crafts & Experiences
by Warner Shedd

Mention bats to most kids and they will immediately tell you that bats are blind. Don't pick up that toad because it will give you warts - right? What most kids know about wildlife is stranger than, well, the fiction that it is! With awesome tales, facts and amusing anecdotes to make activities meaningful and fun, Warner Shedd's thoughtful approach fills children with wonder and respect for the creatures with whom they share this planet.

160 pages, 11 x 8 1/2, with illustrations, range maps
Quality paperback, $12.95

THE KIDS' BOOK OF CRAZY CONCOCTIONS
100 Mysterious Mixtures for Science, Art, & Craft Fun
by Jill Frankel Hauser

Mix it, stretch it, knead it, squish, squash, mush, and mash - however it's done, kids are bound to have endless hours of fun and learning as they concoct the craziest things. Hauser inspires kids with scientific concoctions including secret mixtures for mysterious gooblek, bouncing bubbles, egg magic, invisible ink, dancing raisins, and walking water. Plus sections that answer curious kids' questions while adding to the fun!

160 pages, 11 x 8 1/2, over 300 illustrations
Quality paperback, $12.95

TALES ALIVE!
Ten Multicultural Folk Tales with Art, Craft & Creative Experiences
by Susan Milord

Award-winning author, Susan Milord brings ten folk tales from around the world to life with a myriad of exciting, relevant hands-on activities. *Tales Alive!* will lock these universal stories into the hearts and minds of children for many years to follow. Includes wondrous stories from Native America, Australia, Argentina, China, and Russia, and many other countries. A virtual feast of fun!

160 pages, 8 1/2 x 11, full-color illustrations
Quality paperback, $14.95

SUGAR-FREE TODDLERS
Over 100 Recipes
by Susan Watson

Give your toddlers the gift of lifelong healthy eating habits and a great start on good health by getting the sugar out of their diets now. Susan Watson doesn't just pay lip service to the idea of "sugar-free" - she shows you how to take refined sugars out of your children's mouths. Over 100 recipes packed with good nutrition and great taste, not empty calories. Plus over 200 popular commercial products such as peanut butters and cereals are rated for sugar content.

176 pages, 8 1/4 x 7 1/4, illustrations
Quality paperback, $9.95

GOLDE'S HOMEMADE COOKIES
by Golde Soloway

Over 50,000 copies of this marvelous cookbook have been sold. Now it's in its second edition with 135 of the most delicious cookie recipes imaginable. *Publishers Weekly* says, "Cookies are her chosen realm and how sweet a world it is to visit." You're sure to agree!

176 pages, 8 1/4 x 7 1/4, illustrations
Quality paperback, $8.95

COUNTRY SUPPERS from Uphill Farm
by Carol Lowe-Clay

Gather around the kitchen table, the fireplace, or your favorite picnic spot and enjoy the simple pleasures of the evening meal. With Carol Lowe-Clay's newest collection of country recipes, you'll experience authentic farmhouse cooking that will nourish the body and the spirit. For years, the welcoming aromas of wholesome suppers and pungent, spiced cobblers and pies filled the kitchen at Uphill Farm. Now you, too, can enjoy the warmth and flavors of these exceptionally delicious foods.

160 pages, 8 x 10, illustrations and photographs
Quality paperback, $10.95

Easy-to-Make TEDDY BEARS & All the Trimmings
by Jodie Davis

Now you can make the most lovable, huggable, plain or fancy teddy bears imaginable, for a fraction of store-bought costs. Step-by-step instructions and easy patterns drawn to actual size for large, soft-bodied bears, quilted bears, and even jointed bears. Plus patterns for clothes, accessories—even teddy bear furniture!

208 pages, 8 1/2 x 11, illustrations and patterns
Quality paperback, $13.95

Easy-To-Make CLOTH DOLLS & All the Trimmings
by Jodie Davis

Jodie Davis turns her many talents to making the most adorable and personable cloth dolls imaginable. With her expert directions and clear full-sized patterns, anyone can create these instant friends for a special child or friend. Includes seven 18-inch dolls like Santa, Raggedy Ann, and a clown; a 20-inch baby doll plus complete wardrobe; a 25-inch boy and girl doll plus a wardrobe including sailor suits; and 10 dolls from around the world including a Japanese kimono doll and Amish dolls. Absolutely beautiful and you can do it!

224 pages, 8 1/2 x 11, illustrations and patterns
Quality paperback, $13.95

To Order:

At your bookstore or order directly from Williamson Publishing. We accept Visa and MasterCard (please include number and expiration date), or send check to:

Williamson Publishing Company
Church Hill Road, P.O. Box 185
Charlotte, Vermont 05445
Toll-Free phone orders with credit cards: 1-800-234-8791

Please add $2.50 for postage per total order. Satisfaction is guaranteed or full refund without questions or quibbles.